Promoting British Values in the Early Years

D1556533

Promoting British Values in the Early Years explores what is meant by British values and how these can be promoted in the Early Years Foundation Stage (EYFS). The book encourages practitioners to reflect on their own attitudes and beliefs and highlights the importance of parents, children and practitioners working together to create inclusive communities. It also examines how and why it is important to foster a sense of belonging, provide inspiration and promote positive attitudes in order to improve outcomes for children.

With case studies and useful links to the EYFS, this book will help readers to nurture children's sense of identity and support them in becoming responsible citizens, celebrating diversity and valuing different cultures, customs and practices. It offers practical guidance on how to develop children's understanding of liberty and democracy, and a mutual tolerance and respect for different faiths and beliefs.

This book will be of interest to Early Years practitioners and primary school teachers, as well as undergraduates studying relevant Early Years and Childhood Studies courses. It is also relevant to parents of young children.

Julia Maria Gouldsboro is an Early Years Consultant and Lecturer for the Foundation Degree in Early Years at North Hertfordshire College, affiliated with the University of Hertfordshire, UK.

Promoting British Values in the Early Years

How to Foster a Sense of Belonging

Julia Maria Gouldsboro

Routledge
Taylor & Francis Group

LONDON AND NEW YORK

First published 2018
by Routledge
2 Park Square, Milton Park, Abingdon, Oxon OX14 4RN

and by Routledge
711 Third Avenue, New York, NY 10017

Routledge is an imprint of the Taylor & Francis Group, an informa business

British Library Cataloguing-in-Publication Data
A catalogue record for this book is available from the British Library

Library of Congress Cataloging-in-Publication Data
A catalog record for this book has been requested

ISBN: 978-1-138-63613-2 (hbk)
ISBN: 978-1-138-63614-9 (pbk)
ISBN: 978-1-315-20616-5 (ebk)

Typeset in Optima
by Apex CoVantage, LLC

Contents

Acknowledgements

Many people have been supportive and helped me to complete this book. My sincere thanks to them all.

I would particularly like to thank Routledge for their kindness and support. A special mention to Sarah Richardson and Annamarie Kino, Aiyana Curtis and Clare Ashworth.

Special thanks go to my parents. Although they are no longer with me, I hope they are proud of my achievements. They taught me from a very young age to be respectful and tolerant and I hope I have been.

A great big thank you to my children, Ryan, Conor and Ciara; they are my inspiration. They have cared for me and supported me as much as I have cared and supported them and have been there every step of the way.

I would also like to extend grateful thanks to my family, especially my sister Ann Conway and my cousin John Walsh, who gave me support throughout the writing of the book.

Thank you to Ciara Gouldsboro for illustrating the book with photos from a local setting and thanks to the manager Debbie Murphy, staff, parents, families and children of Parkside Pre-School in Chingford, North East London. They welcomed me into their wonderful, inclusive setting and showed how they celebrate diversity effectively. A warm thank you extends also to Christobel Cousins, the head teacher of Lilleshall Primary School in Shropshire and Maria Hogan, head of year 6 and religious education consultant, for insights into how British values can be promoted in practice.

Introduction
British values in practice — fostering a sense of belonging in the Early Years

The concept of British values in practice requires an ethos inherent in settings and communities that fosters tolerance and respect for each other. These are the qualities that already underpin the Early Years curriculum framework, legislation and policies. The main emphasis to consider is to provide a curriculum that enables children to thrive in an environment of positivity and safety where they learn to grow into responsible and caring individuals. Ensuring that children, from a young age, learn how to express themselves in a fair and sensitive way, whilst respecting other views and opinions, is necessary for them to successfully achieve a sense of democracy. This requires an understanding of fairness and a sense of right and wrong:

> No one can learn tolerance in a climate of irresponsibility, which does not produce democracy. Tolerance requires respect, discipline, and ethics.
>
> (Freire 2005: 77)

It advocates a sense of knowing when children need to be protected from extreme forms of behaviour that may present a danger to their development, growth, and attitudes on how they view the world and each other. The common inspection framework (Ofsted 2015a) informed Early Years settings of the need to produce and implement safeguarding procedures that protected children from exploitation and radicalisation from extreme groups in society. This has been addressed through the Prevent duty guidance. It also introduced the concept of British values and supported settings with examples of how to promote these values through the curriculum so that a positive sense of belonging and identity emerges from those who live and work in Britain.

To effectively promote British values and adhere to the Prevent duty guidance, practitioners need a clear, detailed understanding of safeguarding requirements and a transparent definition of what is meant by British values.

The topics discussed in this book are as follows:

Identity: understanding and taking ownership of identity

The reader is asked to examine and reflect on the definition and understanding of British values. Britain needs to understand its identity and its citizens need to feel that they belong. It is paramount when educating young children that practitioners promote a positive sense of identity and build up self-esteem and self-worth if the future generation wishes to successfully and effectively celebrate diversity, whilst respecting and tolerating differences. This is not a new concept. Many theorists, such as Bowlby, examine the importance of secure attachments, and Goleman refers to this development as emotional intelligence. The best way that this can be achieved is by following legislation that ensures every child matters. Unfortunately, at times, children have been at risk of discrimination and harm. Legislation has tried to combat stereotyping and discriminatory practice by addressing these concerns and having in place rules and laws that are adhered to and above all accepted by society. The concept of British values in practice needs clear and succinct rules for it to be successful.

Safeguarding: the Prevent duty guidance

The Counter Terrorism and Security Act 2015 highlights the responsibility of all those who work or have contact with children to be alert and aware of how children can be drawn in to terrorism, and so this book reflects on the Prevent duty guidance and its impact on practice, safeguarding our most vulnerable children. It asks practitioners to be alert to children's behaviour that may give cause for concern. The Channel duty guidance (https://www.gov.uk/Channel_Duty_Guidance_April_2015.pdf) is an early intervention strategy that supports children and is an extension of safeguarding laws. It is specific to the individual vulnerability of each case. But the Prevent duty guidance has been accused of scaremongering and limiting itself to one form of extremism, which has had a negative effect on groups in society. This book reflects on the different types of extremism and violence that children may be susceptible to from an early age and the importance of working together to support those children identified at risk.

Values and attitudes

For practitioners to be truly good role models to the young generation, they need to be reflective practitioners. They need to evaluate the impact of their attitudes and behaviour when supporting diversity, keeping children safe from extremism and combating stereotyping. Reflecting on our own values and attitudes is a fundamental starting point because, unless we are secure in ourselves and what we value, then it will be difficult to translate this for our youngest children. This book considers the wider context of the practitioner's own values and attitudes and how it can impact on practice. It reflects on the need for honest information to be accessible and available to the practitioner. It also emphasises the importance of being a positive role model and facilitator for all children, supporting them in effectively developing a positive self-esteem and self-worth. At the same time, it is important for practitioners to understand they will not have all the answers but can and should acknowledge all the different questions that come to light on reflection.

The responsibility of the whole community

British values are not only the responsibility of practitioners and professionals that work in educational settings. It goes further than this. It involves parents and the whole community. This book discusses the responsibility of the whole community and defines it as being a meaningful neighbour, ensuring children grow and develop into responsible citizens of the future, understanding that they belong to a community and so their actions will have an impact on the community.

Examples of practice

Finally, by demonstrating how British values in practice can be effective through the curriculum, the ethos behind those values asks practitioners to have a thorough understanding of what it means to be a competent, reflective practitioner. Examples of practice ensure that children from an early age are learning to follow the British values of tolerance, rule of law, individual liberty and democracy to become respectful, caring and responsible citizens. The only effective way practitioners can do this is to find out what we have in common, whilst respecting uniqueness.

When referring to 'practitioners' throughout this book, this is defined as all Early Years professionals, trainers, students, teachers, nursery staff, childminders and all who work and care for children or who are studying to achieve a qualification to work and care for young children.

2 Defining British values
Identity

British values should be a proclamation of what binds us together as a nation. It is paramount that it is accepted as a positive phrase that identifies the rules and values that are adhered to in Britain. In accepting these rules and values practitioners will ultimately help achieve a successful and tolerant society. To accept these rules and values, everyone needs to feel part of the community and the rules and values need to be fair. Society needs to voice opinions to ensure these rules and values continue to be fair. This includes equipping our youngest members of the community with the skills needed, from an early age, to realise that freedom of expression is acceptable but comes with responsibilities.

> All morality consists in a system of rules and the essence of all morality is to be sought for in the respect which the individual acquires for these rules.
>
> (Piaget 1965:1)

The role of the Early Years practitioner is to encourage tolerance and respect for each other from a very early age. Having a successful, enabling environment that supports a generation to feel good about themselves and to care and respect each other ensures that children will celebrate their uniqueness, have a clear sense of belonging and develop a self-respect as well as a positive attitude towards each other. By having clear rules to follow, it ensures children learn to cooperate and interact within these boundaries.

The term 'British values' is a statement that demands the involvement of the whole country. It asks the country to stand together and agree on a set of rules and principles that endeavour to create a fair and equal society. In Early Years' settings, it asks the practitioners and professionals that work with children to have these values as a firm foundation when supporting children in their development. This firm foundation starts with dialogue, which develops into conversations, extends to decision making and grows into freedom to express opinions in a responsible way.

Dialogue with children

It is imperative that practitioners are in a dialogue with children from an early age. Before the learning of knowledge can take place, children always need to share and learn how to work together, to feel confident to explore and make sense of the world. They need opportunities to feel part of the world through dialogue (Brodie 2014). Children have a voice. Children have a right to be heard. They have the right to contribute to decisions that affect them. Paulo Freire (1921–1997) interprets education as a dialogue. He believes dialogue involves respect. It should not involve one person acting for another, but rather people working with each other (Freire 2005). As practitioners, there is an essential agreement that there is a need to promote tolerance, to listen to each other and to have a set of values that, as a nation, are agreed and shared. There is also a constant need to talk and discuss, reflecting on what is successful and what needs to change.

Children need opportunities to engage in dialogue and learn the skill of successful dialogue so that it is understood and accepted that their views and opinions matter. As they grow and develop, this will enable them to feel part of an ongoing dialogue of what works or doesn't work for the society that they feel part of and belong to. Dialogue is the foundation that a democracy is built on and continuous dialogue should guarantee rules are fair and continue to be fair. Legislation in education safeguards children so that they can find a voice.

Children will have conversations with the adults that surround them and so will be influenced in their perceptions from the adults' perceptions and experiences. A child's understanding of self is 'interwoven with the society and culture to which they belong' (Park and King 2003: 1). Dialogue opens the channels of communication and ensures that everyone perceives British values as effective, meaningful and relevant to them.

The importance of identity

For dialogue to be successful, there is a need to have a clear understanding of identity. Children will develop a positive image of themselves and a sense of identity if they feel that they belong. This means the practitioner must know how they can promote an inclusive, positive ethos in the Early Years curriculum. A clear identity enables children to feel confident to contribute to the democracy through dialogue and grow into responsible citizens in the future.

Defining British values

The term 'British values' was introduced to define identity and focus on what we have in common. It lays the foundations for the rules of the nation that should be accepted and followed by everyone. However, the word 'British' seems to cause many problems and some find the term 'parochial, patronising and arrogant' (Rosen 2014). Many interpret it as a political ploy and alarming. In a recent article 'Childhood, Curriculum, Early Years, Education Policy' Jenny Robson (2015) comments that there is an underhanded reason for the language and comments that it could be construed with suspicion.

> Fundamental British values are an attempt by government to articulate a set of values within a broad anti-terrorism strategy; defined as democracy, the rule of law, individual liberty and mutual respect and tolerance for those with different faiths and beliefs.
>
> (Robson 2015)

Some have interpreted it completely wrong and, in a tokenistic way, rushed out to buy the poster of the black taxi or the red bus. 'Promoting British values is not about celebrating stereotypical British traditions and institutions; it is about encouraging the people of Britain to share a set of values that promote tolerance, respect and community cohesion' (Sargent 2016: 9).

Goddard (2016) argues that it should be defined as 'human' values, believing that referring to it as 'British values' has the opposite effect of inclusion and instead creates a divide.

Many communities that have settled in Britain may not define themselves as British or may not be perceived or accepted as part of the British community. There seems to be a confusion regarding who belongs and identifies with Britain, and there are many opinions as to who is accepted as British. For dialogue to be successful, clarity is needed on identity.

Is the identity of Britain multicultural?

History has uncovered many incidences of struggles that have enabled Britain to grow into a nation that hopefully respects and tolerates difference. Many of our European neighbours would describe Britain as multicultural, and this should be welcomed as a positive description. However, the message of multiculturalism, at times, did not have the positive effect it was supposed to have. Some saw it as a form of tokenism and activities in the curriculum around schools demonstrated this with minimal effort.

Britain has always been a diverse society made up of many ethnic groups, religions, cultures and races. The British Isles itself is made up of Irish, English, Welsh and Scottish communities that have very different customs and traditions. Vikings and Romans settled in this country. And many continue to settle in this country and make it their home.

When Britain hosted the Olympics in 2012, it was very keen to portray itself as multicultural. The Olympics bid portrayed images of multiculturalism in a positive light. But this soon changed when immigration became a scapegoat for the problems facing the UK and after the bombing of 7/7 there was a realisation that rejection and isolation was still felt by those that had made Britain their home and had grown up in the same communities they felt rejected and often despised by. Such rhetoric is typified by William Pfaff, writing in *The Observer* just a month after the attacks; in an article headed 'A monster of our own making', he writes, 'these British bombers are a consequence of a misguided and catastrophic pursuit of multiculturalism' (2005).

Defining Britain as multicultural therefore had a knock-on effect. It could be accused of having the opposite effect of inclusion and instead isolated groups. It could also be argued that Britain has failed in defining itself as multicultural. The events in Park View School in Birmingham, known as the Trojan Horse, saw extremists try to infiltrate the school with radical views. The widely reported problem at Park View was that the school became separated from British society and failed to instil a sense of belonging in a national community increasingly defined by multi-faith, multicultural values. It concluded that 'there was no one term that showed a sense of togetherness' (Oldham 2014).

The events highlight that, while there is a place to respect and celebrate diversity, there is an urgent need for common strands to be entwined so that everyone feels part of the same community. Uniqueness and identity can be varied but ultimately common rules that surround peoples' differences need to be agreed upon.

Being defined as multicultural is not enough. There is a definite place for multiculturalism but there is an even more urgent place for identity and a common bond. There are three descriptions of identity that need to be accepted if democracy and effective dialogue is to be successful.

There is a need to accept personal identity, national identity and shared identity.

Personal identity

Identity is important from birth. Knowing that they belong to a family enables children from a very young age to develop self-confidence, and self-worth. Children need to develop a positive self-image and be happy and confident in who they are, and to successfully flourish and boost their self-esteem.

> Because of experiences of being secure and cared for, a baby becomes confident and strengthens his (*or her*) identity.
>
> (Dowling 2013: 27)

From an early age, children want to make sense of the world and want to know who they are and be accepted for who they are. They need to have that sense of belonging so they can learn to be 'resilient, capable and self-assured' (DfE 2014b). Children need to have opportunities to talk with others, to celebrate together and to learn about each other to understand who they are and where they belong.

Through social interactions with others, children gradually construct their ideas of who they are.

(Schaffen and Ochi 1986 from Park and King 2003)

If children do not feel accepted, they will grow up feeling isolated or rejected by the nation that they live in and have made their home in. They may develop what Goleman describes as an emotional malaise (Goleman 1998) that will have a negative effect on their emotional intelligence.

Personal identity is what defines you as a person and includes your ethnicity, culture, race, faith and beliefs. Personal identity is not antagonistic or confrontational to national identity.

National identity

Having a sense of belonging to a community ensures that an identity provides a powerful means of defining and locating individual selves in the world and understand 'who we are' in the wider world. There is a need for us to understand that we all have a unique and personal identity but we also have a national identity that defines where we were born. Being British means accepting that Britain is made up of many different cultures, races and religions that may have been born in Britain, but this is only one aspect of belonging. In his book *A National Identity* (1993), Anthony Smith explains that it is understandable when we reflect on the history and experiences of so many that there is a feeling of not belonging and those who do not consider themselves British. Many raise up visions of the National Front, an extreme organisation with extreme views on races and cultures, discriminating against anyone who is not white British as an outsider; even those who are white but may have a different accent or different culture are rejected. Many see the term 'British' excluding a generation of those who were born here but are perceived as not British based solely on the colour of their skin or their religion. It is important to under-stand the anger that many people feel and the negativity they experience that makes them feel outcast enough to become radicalised. If this is fostered from a young age, for example, telling a child (explicitly or implying) that they are different because of their colour, religion, accent, parents, or even the food they bring to school, then it will foster a sense of 'otherness', that they are different and 'un-British' (Smith 1993).

If adults feel angry, they often act on this anger, but if children feel angry they may internalise it, becoming isolated, and feelings of isolation breed contempt. If children are vulnerable, if they feel isolated and not part of a community, they will begin to internalise these feelings to interpret them to mean that they are worthless and they will develop a poor self-esteem. And when an individual or a group shows them any atten-tion, they are consumed with the fact that at least someone seems to care. When it turns out to be a group with extremely negative opinions and assumptions the child may not be able to walk away as they may feel that those in the group are the only ones that have shown them any attention, even if it is negative.

Children from a very early age, therefore, need to feel that they belong and they need to belong to a positive community that shows care and understanding towards them. Making children feel like outsiders will have a negative effect on their behaviour. There have always been different ways to make groups feel like an 'other', whether this was due to their religion, their customs, food or even their voices.

National identity can easily be stereotyped and perceived as all eating a supposed national dish or following the same customs and traditions. National identity may follow the same customs and traditions but may celebrate them in a variety of ways. National identity includes a variety of personal, unique identities that make a positive and vibrant contribution to Britain.

The community of British people that were born here have come from many different cultures that immigrated to Britain and settled here. The second generation of immigrants are British by birth but also have an ethnicity that is positive and improves the national identity, making it vibrant, unique and worth celebrating.

Many people still come to Britain and bring with them culture and customs that can easily be embraced if they are not contrary to British values.

Shared identity

A shared identity is possibly the most important definition to understand. If personal identity makes us unique and national identity defines where we began our life at birth, shared identity brings us together as a nation. Shared identity includes those who may not have been born in Britain but live in Britain or wish to make it their home. This identity needs us to reflect on the past and current attitudes to belonging and acceptance. Shared identity perceives British identity as respecting personal identity, accepting national identity and understanding shared identity, which means following the same set of rules but at the same time allowing freedom of expression within those rules, allowing uniqueness, tolerating and respecting others and respecting difference. With the introduction of British values, there is a step in the right direction if we take it on wholeheartedly and include all types of identity that make up Britain. It is also important to share this positive outlook of personal identity, national identity and common identity with the youngest members of society for them to have a clear understanding of acceptable and unacceptable behaviour and develop a positive attitude and appropriate responses to the many people that make up Britain today.

Learning from the past

The lack of a shared identity may be the fault of history. And so, before understanding the present and preparing a generation for a positive future, practitioners need to reflect and come to terms with the past; apologise, forgive and learn lessons that should give a more positive outlook on life.

Our upbringing, values and attitudes all have an impact, directly or indirectly, on how we perceive community. If views are negative or based on bad experiences, it is important to consider how this impacts on practice and belief in the core values. Sadly, the circumstances of many events may lead us to think that the concept of British values has come at a time when, as a nation, we do not want to care for everyone but want to limit ourselves to a few. It may be perceived that the values we have in common only serve communities within Britain. Rejecting immigrants in Britain, or being abusive to communities that have made their home in Britain, sends out the message that we are narrow and judgmental in our perception of who belongs. At times, the country has welcomed immigration but often stories or people's experiences have been far from positive.

Many communities of people who were born in Britain feel that the sense of national identity has been lost. They may remember Britain from a long time ago and that Britain is portrayed with fond memories. It may be conceived that the Britain they recognised has been swallowed up by too many differences. This sometimes alienates groups that have joined Britain and causes unrest and a false sense of nationalism. The answer is not to alienate groups solely on the grounds of race or culture. These same cultures that have been rejected or feel isolated add a vibrancy to our national identity and have worked hard to create the Britain we have today.

Past experiences also play a great part in how different communities, races or cultures are perceived and often appear in a negative light. History has shown us that negativity about someone's ethnic origin or culture breeds contempt and allows anger and assumptions to grow leading to discrimination, racism and stereotyping. Sadly, events in history and in Britain often showed discrimination against communities purely based on the colour of their skin, their language or accent. These groups were not accepted as British and some are still working to try and be accepted even though they may have contributed positively to the growth of Britain, made their home here and believe in the values and ethos of the country.

In the late 1950s and early 1960s, signs in guest houses and pubs reflected a negative attitude towards the workforce of Irish labourers and skilled people from the Caribbean that were invited to work in Britain. The date 22 June 1948 has become an important landmark in the history of modern Britain. The ship *Windrush* brought many Caribbeans to work in the UK by the invitation of the British government. It has come to symbolise many of the changes that have taken place here. Caribbean migrants have become a vital part of British society and, in the process, transformed important aspects of British life. In 1948, Britain was just beginning to recover from the Second World War. Housing was a huge problem and stayed that way for the next two decades. There was plenty of work, but the Caribbeans who were working in construction were not welcomed at many establishments that offered accommodation or entertainment and leisure.

Irish labour was also used to build in the UK, and again the experience of many Irish workers was negative and brutal, with racist remarks about their knowledge or understanding.

Signs displayed included:

- No Blacks
- No Irish
- No dogs

And yet, many British buildings and institutions grew successfully because of the hard work of the immigrants that came to this country. As practitioners and educators of Early Years, our mantra is to promote positivity and a future generation that is respectful, open to diversity and part of change. For this to be successful, lessons from history need to be learnt and resolved.

It is worth considering that British values can be found in the foundations and ethos of many different cultural groups that fought for fairness, free speech and respect of traditions. The rapper Akala explains in a YouTube clip that we are taught a distorted version of history, which erases serious political struggle (*The Guardian* 2016). He adds that, when defining British values, we should not make the mistake that these values came from the aristocracy or well-known figures in history such as Winston Churchill alone but from 'the relentless activism that secured for us the fragile freedoms we have today'. He argues that there is a need to acknowledge movements such as the suffragette movement or the traditions of the Notting Hill carnival that began as a message against racism, or the work of William Cuffay, a disabled Black man who founded the Chartist movement for the freedom of speech, as part of British history to be proud of and which contributed to the authentic foundations for British values (Every Generation n.d.).

Many prominent figures from different ethnic groups that settled in Britain and viewed themselves as British made the firm foundations that are referred to as British values today. Therefore, the term British is inclusive if the work and struggle of all who helped to form Britain are acknowledged.

Shared identity and its part in British values

British values are based on values that were fought for throughout history by many cultures and races who believed in working together to create a positive and fair Britain.

The concept 'British values' should be a title that brings us together and lays the foundations for the ethos and teaching of the young generation. It enshrines what we have in common. But at the same time, the very essence of British values celebrates what makes us unique.

The importance of identity for young children

Young children need to have opportunities and experiences that make them confident and proud of their individual identity but also have a clear understanding of their national and shared identity so they can make sense of the wider world and hopefully see that world as inclusive and respectful of uniqueness.

Britain is made up of small individual groups with a variety of cultures, races and religions and needs an inclusive and protective umbrella to stand under that gives a clear defined identity. At the same time, there is a need to celebrate and proclaim diversity and, in doing so, realise that diversity is our strongest bond and ultimately defines our Britishness.

Links to practice

Children need to feel that they belong from a very early age for them to develop emotionally and feel positive about themselves. They need to have a clear personal identity

Figure 2.1 Children, from a very early age, need to feel that they belong to a positive community that shows care and understanding towards them. An inclusive and protective umbrella to stand under enables children to feel welcome and part of Britain.

but also accept the identities of others and realise what binds us together, finding out what we have in common and celebrating this commonality. Children need role models who also have a positive sense of identity and belonging. British values are not about old traditions or limited to a few in our society. It is accepting the many diverse, cultural, communities that make up Britain and continue to provide a positive contribution to Britain. It is about accepting this contribution and diversity in a positive light. As practitioners, it is vital that uniqueness is celebrated. Each child is an individual with a background rooted in culture, traditions or religion. This needs to be celebrated. Practitioners need to acknowledge the variety of cultures and celebrate differences. At the same time, there is a need to celebrate community and what makes us work and grow together within the rules and boundaries that we follow. This leads us to accepting an honest and genuine national identity.

My own reflection on my identity

I consider my ethnicity as Irish but my nationality as British. Growing up, my family was often rejected by members of the community that called themselves British.

During the bombing of the Old Bailey in 1973, our windows were smashed and our family called 'Irish scum'. Abuse was hurled at us. My dad worked as a cleaner at the Old Bailey and, during that time, was regarded with suspicion purely because he was Irish. This made me feel very angry and alienated from a very early age. It made me like all things Irish and dislike things considered English.

My dad felt that, even though he was angry or upset at times, change would come through education and time and knowledge would change people's perceptions.

I did not feel this for a long time and instead felt very angry.

However, I received a good education. Most of my teachers and lecturers that supported me were kind, supportive and positive. My experiences as a teacher were mainly positive. My experiences as a parent and part of a community were positive and welcoming.

When I first started teaching, it was very important to me that I supported all children in my care, that I respected their backgrounds and did not make judgements.

As a teacher, I was working in a school in Hackney when the term multiculturalism was first introduced. It was received with mixed responses.

We celebrated diversity and tried to be inclusive in practice.

This has constantly been reflected in education, and promoting British values extends the need to celebrate difference but at the same time find out what we have in common or should have in common.

Sadly, my experience is more common than we would like to believe and, unfortunately, many children and adults still feel isolated or rejected by communities because of the colour of their skin, their religion or culture. It would be naïve to think that times have changed as some communities still feel under attack.

And yet, by living in or working in Britain, we have in common a British identity, a desire to be here and a hope for the future.

Britain needs a new, clearly defined and honest identity

Britain needs to acknowledge that being British must include what for many years was considered unBritish. We need to change our perception of Britain. And the only way this can be achieved successfully and effectively is by all strands of our community focusing on the positive. This includes the news, media, social media, local communities and all walks of society, but especially Early Years settings. If we are to teach our young that we all belong and our society is a tolerant society, then we need to truly believe it. What is needed is to find shared experiences and what we have in common, whilst understanding that every child is unique.

Pugh and Duffy (2014: 184) argue that national identity and democracy is more than sharing a common set of values. 'It goes further in the sense that there is a desire to have mutual respect and tolerance for the vibrancy and differences that walk side by side with the shared identity' (Pugh and Duffy 2014: 184). Osler and Starkey (2005) find the best description when discussing identity is to refer to it as 'cosmopolitan citizenship', which they believe encompasses citizenship learning as a whole and provides us with a better understanding of national identity.

By proclaiming our identity, there should be a new approach to how we perceive ourselves as a nation and we must consider the term British values as a step in the right direction. As practitioners, there is a need to understand and accept this if we are to be successful and competent educators of the youngest members of society. Practitioners should believe in an environment of tolerance and accept the uniqueness of each other if they are imparting to children the importance of living in harmony. Practitioners need clear and focused principles and aims as children need to learn from a very early age skills that will equip them to live in a society that is welcoming, tolerant and has a sense of right and wrong.

Modern Britain needs an understanding and acceptance of a variety of identities: personal, national and shared identity

Being British in the twenty-first century means moving forward in our thinking. Being British means recognising that we live in Britain, accept the rules, and respect the ethnic identity or characteristics that people choose to describe themselves as. It does not make people less British if their personal identity, for example their ethnicity, is different from the nation they live in. it also means accepting those many communities that contribute to Britain and adhere to the laws of the nation. Every society has rules and values and principles that they follow. When referring to values as British, as a nation, we are proclaiming that these are the core values of our country.

If you are born in Britain, then it is obvious that you are a British citizen. However, to have a truly national identity that is British means accepting the British values in practice. It also asks for acceptance that backgrounds may be rooted in other cultures and this makes up your personal identity but does not make you a lesser citizen. But Britishness goes beyond this definition. If you make Britain your home and abide by the rules of democracy, respect for others, liberty and the law, then you are welcome to define yourself as British. You may define yourself as British and Italian, British Greek, British Irish or British and Muslim. You may define yourself as British and Black or a British Jew. You may define yourself as Polish, living in Britain, or Turkish and living in Britain. You have a right to define your ethnic identity as something different because it should not be antagonistic to you as a British person. A person's ethnic identity is their personal identity. Shared identity goes further in its definition as it welcomes the ethos of Britain.

Being British means respecting that one person may identify themselves as totally different from another person but they are ultimately British because they believe and want to promote the core British values which are:

Figure 2.2 Diversity is our strongest bond.

- Democracy
- Rule of law
- Individual liberty
- Mutual respect and tolerance of different faiths and beliefs

Understanding this concept leads us to realise that diversity is our strongest bond and British values is the glue that keeps us together.

How do people in Britain describe themselves today?

Finally, I have added some personal stories of how some people in the community define themselves.

The 'cosmopolitan citizens' as described by Pugh and Duffy (2014) need to be apparent and celebrated in Early Years settings.

Visiting a local pre-school in Chingford, North East London, I asked the staff and parents if they felt part of Britain and if they interpreted the phrase in a positive light.

Cosmopolitan citizens

The staff are from a variety of backgrounds but all consider themselves British. Dzulietta Constantinou, a nursery practitioner from Estonia, explains that she settled in Britain in 2002. As she decorates the Christmas tree with the children, she tells me that she feels very much part of British society and remarks that Britain 'feels like home'.

Irene Coppeard, deputy manager and special needs coordinator, has worked in this setting for over 20 years. She remembers the area when it was predominately white middle class and feels the different cultures that now make up the community are a positive strength of the community. She explains that everyone has a value and that it is important to respect parents and reassure them that their child is unique and that the setting does not see children as the same but welcomes the differences and uniqueness. She wishes that every setting could have that outlook. However, she feels that some communities are more tolerant and some have a lack of knowledge, or sometimes they have fear or they don't want to offend so they don't ask about celebrations or traditions.

Oya Salih has recently joined the setting and feels the setting puts the children first. She supports children with specific needs and believes it is vital to care for children. Oya can speak Turkish and English and explains that this is a great help and support to Turkish parents who may find English difficult at times. She has also taught the staff phrases to help settle the children by using familiar words in Turkish.

Sem Karamehmet agrees but also adds that she tells parent that Turkish is used to bridge a gap but English is the language that they support all children in acquiring.

As safeguarding officer for the setting, she has delivered training to parents and staff so that signs of abuse are understood. Recently, she gave a workshop on safeguarding and used scenarios for staff to understand the new Prevent duty.

One such scenario was about signs to be alert and concerned over if there was a suspicion of female genital mutilation (FGM), and she feels this helps enormously if they talk about these cases together.

Doris has been in Britain for over 40 years and is originally from Canada. She believes that the tone that some people use may imply negativity, even if this may not be the case. British values are a positive thing but could be misinterpreted if the tone is abrupt or interpreted as non-inclusive. She recalls a memory when she first applied for a job and the interviewer exclaimed 'We are a very British firm!'

She remembers that she went away feeling that they did not want her or like her as she was Canadian, and yet she got the job and enjoyed the job for many years. It made her realise that the way that she speaks to parents or children is very important, and she needs to be approachable and polite and pleasant so that they feel welcome and part of the setting.

I spoke to many parents at the setting and asked them if they have a sense of belonging and if they feel that they are British and accepted as British.

Shaun Alexander drops his young child at the pre-school and then goes off to work. He informs me that he feels part of the community of the setting. He also feels British. He adds that every community has 'ups and downs' but the community needs to work together through the rough times.

Dionne Brown agrees and adds that, although she may have had negative experiences in her life growing up, it is the positive ones that count. She believes the setting is very positive and teachers are very approachable. Because her child has settled, she feels settled.

Lily Anne Doherty feels British is a strong word in a positive way, and Emma Waller finds the phrase British values gives us a sense of togetherness and again agrees that British is a strong word. She says true British values can be seen when she meets with all the parents and they are all 'chatting away', whatever the race, colour or faith. She sees Britain as multicultural and this is a positive thing to be proud of.

Lorna Luker is a parent new to the setting and informs me that her child has an extra chromosome (Down's syndrome). She feels that she has been made to feel part of the setting, which is so welcoming and inclusive, and adds that Britain is a multicultural and diverse place and her daughter is definitely part of it.

The parents are from a variety of backgrounds and so are the staff, but what is wonderful to hear and see is the positivity about each other and the setting, how they feel welcome, how they all feel like one family, how they are reassured and happy because their children are safe and how they feel part of this community.

This is British values in practice.

Summary

British values in practice should be a positive term that defines our national identity. But at the same time, it is important to understand how we are all unique in our personal identity. Even within the same culture, the younger generation may have a different perception of their culture than the older generation. It is important to understand the definition of 'British'. It creates a sense of identity that is vital if the future generation is to feel accepted as part of a community. Being British means accepting and respecting how people define themselves. They may define themselves as British Indian, or British Catholic or British Muslim or a Black British Muslim or a young British Greek man. These definitions proclaim what is important and influential in their lives.

The common strand is that we are all British. National identity welcomes personal identity, which consists of the variety of cultures and beliefs that form Britain. It also extends further stating that being part of Britain asks those that have made their home in Britain or wish to settle in Britain to respect and accept the laws and rules of the country knowing that their faith, belief, cultures and customs will be respected if they are not contrary to British values in practice.

When there is a clear understanding of identity and acceptance of difference, when there is a clear set of rules to work within, there can be a clear understanding of what we need to protect children from and what we need to promote to achieve a happy and successful community.

By accepting the many groups that make and contribute to what it means to be British, it enables practitioners and all members of society to become good role models for the younger generation. In Early Years settings, practitioners need to spend time getting to know children, allowing them to talk and be part of decisions in the setting. They need to celebrate their uniqueness and form attachments to the children in their care so that they feel happy and secure. Practitioners need to ultimately understand what is meant by personal identity and national identity and how both need to be entwined together to impact positively on practice. Practitioners need to consider shared identity and welcome families into the communities who settle and make their homes in Britain. Practitioners also need to feel that they belong if they are to truly promote this effectively in practice.

3 Following the rules and values

British values include:

- **Rule of law**
- **Democracy**
- **Individual liberty**
- **Mutual respect and tolerance**

Understanding British values

Rule of law To be a successful democratic society, citizens need to abide by the rules. Rules and laws originate from trying to put right what went wrong in the past. When considering the care, development and safety of children, laws are passed to ensure that every child is protected. The underpinning themes of British Values are not a new concept. The United Nations Convention on the Rights of the Child (UNCRC 2015) has consistently declared the same message of democracy, individual liberty, rule of law and mutual tolerance and respect. The Children Act 2004 introduced Every Child Matters and outlined the five outcomes of being healthy, staying safe, enjoying and achieving, making a positive contribution and achieving economic well-being as crucial to a child's development. The Childcare Act 2006 introduced the Early Years Foundation Stage as a curriculum and had four main themes in supporting a child's development, namely seeing each child as unique, making positive relationships, providing an enabling environment and supporting them in their learning and development. In this chapter, legislation is reflected upon and its impact defined.

UNCRC United Nations Convention on the Rights of the Child

After the Second World War, the UNCRC devised a list of articles that each country in the United Nations would adhere to so that children would have a firm foundation of peace and grow up with tolerance and respect.

Legislation in Britain has firm foundations in the UNCRC. Nonetheless, there is a need to ensure that these rights are adhered to and to continue to keep our youngest children

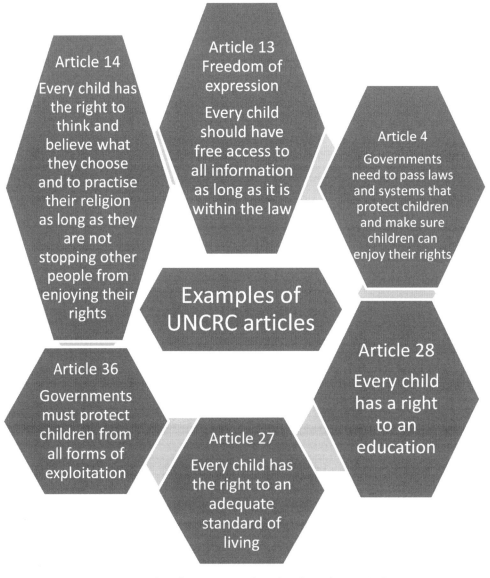

Figure 3.1 Examples of UNCRC articles taken from the UNCRC 1989.

safe, allowing them opportunities to thrive. There is always a necessity to reflect. It is paramount to reflect on history, to report on laws and legislation and to consider the impact of present policies and opinions on the future generation. It is essential that the articles of the UNCRC were not just formulated and then forgotten. Each country that belongs to the United Nations constantly reflects on these articles and ensures that these rights are still upheld.

One way Britain reflects regularly on the rules of the UNCRC is by listening to and reading the reports and findings from non-government organisations (NGO reports). Non-government organisations (NGOs) report on the UNCRC, flagging up issues that the government needs to address. NGOs can submit their own reports, known as 'alternative reports' to the Committee. NGOs generally work in collaboration with one another, and they have a key role in supporting children and young people's views to be heard as part of the government report. Some of the key issues unearthed by NGOs have been in relation to vulnerable children.

> Key issues are addressed in the report including: the effect of austerity on vulnerable groups of children; social and economic inequalities which affect children's access to health, education or adequate standards of living; and the far-reaching implications of planned reforms including the repeal of the Human Rights Act.
>
> (UNCRC 2015)

Many recent NGO reports have concerns for children who arrive in Britain unaccompanied, and many address issues such as exploitation and fear of being drawn into extreme violent groups such as gangs.

The Good Childhood Report 2016 (The Children Society 2016, childrenssociety.org.uk) states that one of the main worries that children have is how safe the local area is and this is clearly linked to their well-being. 'The quality of local facilities, how safe they feel and their experience of local problems are all important. Noisy neighbours and people drinking or taking drugs are the local problems with the strongest links to well-being' (The Children Society 2016). Children are aware of what is around them. They make sense of the world by making sense of the environment and the Good Childhood Report shows that a child's environment has an impact on their confidence. These reports impact on legislation, updating it to include more robust ways to safeguard children.

The Prevent duty guidance and British values have begun to address how to protect vulnerable children. Legislation is another way that ensures children are protected.

Laws are sometimes passed in response to the cruelty inflicted on children. Robust systems are put in place so that it hopefully never happens again. The Children Act 2004 and Every Child Matters paper were in response to the cruelty and subsequent death of Victoria Climbié. The Laming report addressed the need for children to be listened to and Lord Laming found limited conversations with Victoria Climbié as one of the reasons that many failed the child. 'In reality, the conversations with Victoria were limited to little more than "hello, how are you?" The only

Table 3.1 UNCRC articles were put in place so that children would have a firm foundation of peace and grow up with tolerance and respect

Example one **Concern for children**	Example two **Concern for children**	Example three **Concern for children**
The NGOs believe the UK government is prioritising its immigration policy over its obligations to asylum seeking children, and that this results in discriminatory treatment of these children.	Economic exploitation The NGOs stated that there exist limitations for young people in the recently introduced Employment Equality (Age) Regulations (NI) 2006, which does not prohibit age discrimination in service provision.	Sexual exploitation and trafficking The NGOs stated that a central source of information about the numbers of children and young people involved in sexual exploitation does not exist. This has helped the problem to remain a hidden issue with the young people most in need.
Recommendation from report It is recommended that the UK legislate to establish a statutory system of guardianship for all separated children – review legislation governing the employment of children to ensure it adequately protects children and does not discriminate.	**Recommendation from report** Ensure that all children in employment are receiving the same minimum wage as adults – ensure that the employment of children and young people is effectively regulated.	**Recommendation from report** Establish mechanisms for proactively identifying young people at risk of, or experiencing, sexual exploitation; develop multi-agency protocols enabling effective pathways of referral and provision of services – ensure provision of adequately resourced early intervention and intensive support services to address the complex needs of sexually exploited children and young people (including health, mental health, sexual health and relationship counselling, basic education).

Note: Table 3.1 examples adapted from Northern Ireland Assembly (2008).

"assessment" completed involved the writing down of limited and sometimes contradictory information provided by her Aunt Marie Terese Kouao' (Laming 2003). The report also found that childcare services needed to work together more.

> The finding of the inquiry pointed a finger at the failing of individuals and their departments to inform other relevant agencies about the extent of the abuse and the complete lack of empathy and focus on a vulnerable child.
>
> (Laming 2003)

The legislation that followed and notably 'Working Together to Safeguard Children 2015' observed that communicating with children protects them from abuse.

Legislation, and reflections on legislation, is the foundation of the rules and principles when working with children. Legislation surrounding equality and fairness is the basis and starting point for British values and these laws need constantly reflecting on and updating if, as a society, we are to remain fair. Extreme behaviour is not new.

Racism (indirect and direct racism) has led to a great deal of extreme negative behaviour towards certain groups in society. Legislation has historically attempted to resolve conflicts of discrimination and stereotyping and continues this today.

The Race Relations Act (1976), Sex Discrimination Act (1975), Disability Discrimination act (1995), Equal Pay Act (1970) reiterated that discrimination was illegal. The Equality Act of 2010 and the Public-sector equality duty published in April 2011 emphasised the continuous need to treat people fairly and free from discrimination.

> It replaced previous anti-discrimination laws with a single Act, making the law easier to understand and strengthening protection in some situations. It sets out the different ways in which it's unlawful to treat someone.
>
> (Government Equalities Office and Equality and Human
> Rights Commission 2013)

Britain, as a nation, has attempted to respond to racism and discrimination by reflecting on the laws and putting in to practice legislation to combat negative attitudes. At times, this worked effectively. One positive example has been the untiring pursuit from Doreen Lawrence to change legislation on direct and indirect racism. Following the murder of their son Stephen Lawrence in 1993, Doreen and Neville Lawrence claimed that the Metropolitan Police investigation was not being conducted in a professional manner, citing incompetence and racism. In 1999, after years of campaigning, and with the support of many in the community, an inquiry investigated the circumstances of Stephen Lawrence's death. The public inquiry concluded that the Metropolitan Police was 'institutionally racist' and that this was one of the primary causes of their failure to solve the case (Gregory 2015).

As a country, it is paramount to improve on the laws ensuring everyone feels welcome and safe from harm and discrimination. For society to be tolerant, respectful and disciplined, there is a need to constantly review legislation as this is vital to living together cohesively. This should lead to a successful democratic society

Democracy A democracy advocates that everyone should be treated fairly and encouraged to participate in decision making.

Individual liberty describes the importance of self-identity enabling its people to have a voice. It also allows for freedom of expression. However, with freedom of expression or the right to think and believe independently, comes responsibility. This is a value that needs to be at the root of children's early learning. The practitioner needs to understand British values on their level but also on the child's level and how these values are addressed in an age appropriate way. Freedom of expression comes with a responsibility to treat others with fairness and respect. Democracy and individual liberty go hand-in-hand and allow us to question or protest if we feel that laws are unfair or have the opposite effect of bringing us together. As adults, laws allow us to question and protest and to be involved in the decision-making processes.

Links to the Early Years settings

Early Years settings are a central focus to a child's development and the hub of a community. Early Years settings have a tremendous influence on a child's development and so it is imperative for good attachments to be formed from an early age. Practitioners support children, and good practitioners make attachments that say to the child 'I care about you. I will look after you and protect you'.

The policies and procedures in a setting are created from a response to legislation. The policies and procedures show the way, practically, that legislation is followed through the routines of the day. All policies and procedures need to respect all families in the setting and not make assumptions that could be antagonistic. Practitioners also need to be vigilant regarding what to protect children from. They need to know the signs and indicators of abuse and have a clear understanding of groups that could influence children in their behaviour in a negative and extreme way. Practitioners need to keep up to date with training and sharing information so that children are protected if concerns arise. Ultimately, practitioners need to show respect for others and encourage this quality in children if we are to truly follow British values.

Figure 3.2 Good practitioners say to the child 'I care about you. I will look after you and protect you'.

Mutual respect and tolerance

Mutual respect and tolerance ensure that, as a society, we can live in peace, respecting and celebrating our diversity.

> This is the expectation that people of different races, with different faiths, from varying cultural backgrounds and with opposing views and beliefs should be able to live and work together in peace.
>
> (Sargent 2016: 9)

Article 29 of the UNCRC asks us to 'demonstrate tolerance for different ethnicities and religions'. Britain is stating that it is proud to be tolerant and respectful of other faiths, beliefs and cultures.

Summary

Legislation has always put the safety of the child at the forefront of laws and reflected on their success by updating or introducing new laws. Sadly, laws are often updated because children have suffered abuse or torment and there has been a need to reflect on how we can tighten the safety net. The Good Childhood Report 2016 indicated that one of the main areas of concern for children was the local area in which they live being unsafe. NGO reports have also highlighted vulnerable children that need better protection from exploitation. Extremism is a real threat to children and communities. If children feel isolated or rejected or grow up with negative views, they are more than likely to join or accept groups that promote negative attitudes towards the communities that they live in.

Practitioners in the Early Years settings must have in place policies and procedures that are a response to the law and are followed rigorously to keep children from harm. They also need to provide opportunities and experiences for young children to grow and develop a mutual respect and tolerance of each other and foster a sense of belonging. Radicalisation and exploitation of children is a form of abuse that practitioners need to be aware of and to be alert to the procedures to follow if they feel children are being subjected to this form of abuse.

The Prevent duty guidance and British values are responses to an urgency to keep children safe from extremism and violence.

Protecting our identity
Understanding and implementing the Prevent duty guidance

The act of tolerating requires a climate in which limits may be established, in which there are principles to be respected. That is why tolerance is not coexistence with the intolerable. Under an authoritarian regime, in which authority is abused, or a permissive one, in which freedom is not limited, one can hardly learn tolerance.

(Freire 1998: 42)

Any laws passed must ensure that those same laws reflect a tolerant society while protecting society from extreme behaviour that goes against those rules imposed.

Once the term 'British values' is defined and understood, when British values demonstrates it is inclusive and there is a respect for how people define themselves, there will be an understanding of what contradicts this term. Being British and Muslim, for example, should not contradict this term. Being British and black should not contradict this term. Being Irish, Polish or Turkish and working in Britain should not contradict this term. Respect and tolerance for a person's personal identity is linked to respect for national identity, which entails following the rules of that nation. We need a common bond that unites us and this is found in British values.

When a society views some of its communities as 'others' and different in a negative way, barriers form and fear escalates. It is vital that, from legislation and guidance, assumptions or stereotyping do not breed more anxiety and separation when the main aims are to live together peacefully. Stereotyping is a product of fear, which may lead to a climate of fear. Of course, it is vital to stay alert, to be aware of the dangers and be vigilant to new fears and address them so that communities feel safe. However, it is also important not to twist meanings or refer to one group as the cause of all the extremism and yet again follow a destructive negative path, advocating negative opinions against one group in society.

As good role models for the youngest members of society, there is a need be attentive and observant as to how to protect our young. However, there seems to be a fine line between keeping children safe on the one hand and living in a society that is fearful and makes assumptions around fear.

A fear culture can become detrimental to your mind and well-being, as Hermona Soreq, a professor of molecular neuroscience, identified. From research, Professor Soreq concluded that anxiety induced by fear is associated with an increased risk of stroke or heart attacks. Research carried out on 17,000 Israelis found that long-term exposure to the threat of terrorism can elevate people's resting heart rates (ScienceDaily 2014).

Fostering a sense of belonging is vital for everyone to feel part of a society and willing to follow the rules and values of that country. Eradicating stereotypes and discrimination really is the only way forward if we want to promote a welcoming and inclusive society where young people do not feel isolated or rejected. Intervention is also important to relay positive attitudes and inclusivity, but intervention may only come to light if there has been a concern. For this reason, safeguarding is the priority.

Safeguarding children is an enormous responsibility for the practitioner. Policies and procedures must be clear and succinct and every member of staff needs to know what to do if there is a concern.

The introduction of the Prevent duty guidance came into force from the Counter Terrorism and Security Act, which addressed the real fear of terrorism in the twenty-first century. It could be argued that its remit alone may be enough to increase fear but it is a guidance that wishes to prevent and discusses interventions as well as what to do if practitioners have concerns.

The main statement of the Act is simply expressed as the need to 'prevent people from being drawn into terrorism'.

However, the remit shows that the Act does not only focus on terrorism as extreme behaviour; its foundations lay in the real threat of many extreme behaviours and groups. It also considers the dangers this poses to vulnerable children that have been identified by NGO reports.

The Prevent duty guidance has further expanded 'consistent with the provision of safe effective care' to include the importance of recognising children that may be vulnerable to exploitation and extremism and informs the practitioner to undertake training to understand what constitutes extremism (HM Government 2015a: 5).

Factors that may suggest a child is vulnerable may be:

- Children that have had experience of racism or discrimination.
- Children who have a feeling of isolation.
- Children that have lost their identity or do not feel valued.
- It may be apparent in children that have low self-esteem.
- Children that have perceptions of injustice.

It may be these children are victims of bullying or other forms of abuse and so it is important to be cautious and not stigmatise individuals purely because they possess these vulnerabilities.

It is also important to remember that children that may be vulnerable to extremism are not confined to an area or economic background.

Understanding terms used

Radicalisation refers to the process by which a person comes to support terrorism and extremist ideologies associated with terrorist groups.

Prevention in the context of this document means reducing or eliminating the risk of individuals becoming involved in terrorism. Prevent includes but is not confined to the identification and referral of those at risk of being drawn into terrorism and uses the Channel awareness guidance to support vulnerable individuals intervening as early as possible.

Extremism was defined in the Prevent duty guidance (2015) as vocal or active opposition to fundamental British values, including democracy, the rule of law, individual liberty and mutual respect and tolerance of different faiths and beliefs. We also include in our definition of extremism calls for the death of members of our armed forces, whether in this country or overseas.

Terrorism is a response against the rules and laws put forward by a society. If in that society groups are alienated or disagree with the laws imposed, protests follow. If these protests lead to aggression and violence, a line is crossed that puts people at risk.

The Prevent duty guidance should not be perceived as a fear factor, but it could be accused of exactly this and has been interpreted solely on being wary and concerned about the actions of one group. The Prevent duty guidance does not single out one form of extremism but many have read it and interpreted it as referring to only one group. The report by Rights Watch UK in July 2016, an NGO, highlights how it may be having the opposite effect to which it set out to achieve 'by dividing, stigmatizing and alienating segments of the population' (Bowcott and Adams 2016). The Prevent duty guidance has further expanded 'consistent with the provision of safe effective care' to include the importance of recognising children that may be vulnerable to exploitation and extremism and informs the practitioner to undertake training to understand what constitutes extremism.

This guidance should be read in conjunction with other relevant guidance. In England, this includes *Working Together to Safeguard Children*, *Keeping Children Safe in Education* and *Information Sharing: Advice for Professionals Providing Safeguarding Services to Children, Young People, Parents and Carers*. We cannot ignore the fact that children may be susceptible to extremism from an early age from subtle messages they hear or receive. However, it is important not to jump to conclusions or make assumptions

The NGO Rights Watch UK in July 2016 summarises a case identified as the 'Cucumber Case' (Fox 2016).

The Cucumber Case

Teachers who were 'anxious to comply with duties to identify ambiguous apparent risk factors in children' recalled an incident relating to a 4-year-old child. As his mother recounted, her son's nursery called her in and informed her that her son had 'been drawing inappropriate pictures'. The picture of apparent concern was described by her son as a drawing of his father slicing a cucumber: the nursery teacher said she thought the infant had said 'cooker-bomb'. By the time the mother was contacted, her son had already been referred under Prevent – the nursery was contacting her to ask for her signature on a formal referral record.

Reflecting on this situation, it needs to be considered if the setting could have taken various steps to assure themselves as to the child's safety at home.

This case highlights the pressure teachers and staff feel they now work under. It also, possibly, highlights the demand and urgency to report anything that, even when misheard, still starts the roller coaster ride of suspicion.

From this case, it is necessary to reflect on training that is involved in the Prevent duty guidance. It is also important to highlight the value of building relationships with parents and carers. Therefore, it is important to promote tolerance and respect but it needs a framework of rules and laws to abide by within the remit.

Practitioners have a duty to update their knowledge and have a clear and honest understanding of the facts and statistics surrounding the groups that make up the community and the groups within different communities that are considered vulnerable or that the system is failing.

A positive acknowledgement of the many cultures and customs within our community is needed where attention is paid to those that may feel alienated or vulnerable and improve outcomes for those that we are failing.

The true message of the Prevent duty guidance

The Prevent duty guidance puts in place what the police, education and health services need to do if members of a community are not following the rules and are radicalising or exploiting children. **Practitioners should be careful not to assume it only refers to certain groups**, and they also need to understand that, within the rules and laws, there is a place for freedom of expression and healthy debate.

Legislation is constantly updated and reviewed, particularly if something horrendous has happened to a child that makes us want to tighten our laws so that it does not happen again. The death of Victoria Climbié led to the Children Act 2004, and there is now a more robust system in place for agencies to work together when it comes to keeping a child safe from harm.

The Prevent duty guidance has extended the safety net and asks us at times, as practitioners, to think the unthinkable. It is a response from the Security and Terrorism Act 2015 and has identified vulnerable children in our system that may be exposed to extremism. At the same time, it is a guidance that advocates the need to provide a safe but inclusive environment. It refers to strategies such as mentoring and prevention as well as identifying many groups that have the potential to exploit. It explains the role of anyone working in the community such as police, health workers and schools to keep the community safe. There is a specific section advising Early Years workers on their role in safeguarding children.

Early Years settings and the Prevent duty guidance

The government emphasises the need to keep our youngest members of society safe from harm.

'Early Years providers serve arguably the most vulnerable and impressionable members of society' and must remain alert (HM Government 2015a: 10). Because of this statement the Prevent duty guidance needs to form part of our everyday practice. It is extremely important to remember that all forms of exploitation and harmful groups need to be considered.

The Prevent duty guidance defines extremism as 'vocal or active opposition to fundamental British values, including democracy, the rule of law, individual liberty and mutual respect and tolerance of different faiths and beliefs' (DfE 2014a: 13).

It defines extreme groups and explains some of the forms of extremism to be aware of.

Examples of extremism

White supremacist groups

Terrorists associated with the extreme right also pose a continued threat to our safety and security. The white supremacist ideology of extreme right-wing groups has also provided both the inspiration and justification for people who have committed extreme right-wing terrorist acts.

Gang culture

Exploitation can go further and deeper than just particular groups and includes gang culture and bullying. There are many groups in society that feel completely isolated and rejected by the society that they live in. This could be due to poverty or poor education.

It could be because of negative attitudes around them. Often, these young people turn to other extreme groups.

> Gangs often share an identity based either on age, location, ethnicity, peer networks or blood relationships and tend to be hierarchical communities with common interests and shared purposes.
>
> (University of Leicestershire 2006)

The University of Leicester examined the influence of gangs. It realised that children involved with gangs saw gangs as a form of attachment but formed negative attachment.

Why do people join gangs?

Gangs may form due to social exclusion and discrimination. People come together for a sense of safety and belonging. Immigrant populations and those excluded from education or people who have engaged in criminal activities from an early age are particularly at risk of gang involvement. Others may join a gang simply for something to do, seeking protection in numbers, or for reasons of status and peer pressure.

This does not happen straight away, but this is a build-up of anger and isolation from a very young age when extreme views and violence may often be inflicted on gang members. Gang culture may often groom children from a young age by enticing them with rewards and then demanding them to carry out violent or sexual favours to remain as part of the gang.

Muslim extremist groups

> Islamist extremists specifically attack the principles of civic participation and social cohesion. These extremists purport to identify grievances to which terrorist organisations then claim to have a solution.
>
> (HM Government 2015a: 3)

It is paramount to clarify that **extremist groups can be found in all religions** and so it needs to be understood as a threat to safety if views are extreme and go against the core British values.

Has the Prevent duty guidance covered extremism and radicalisation effectively?

To a certain extent, yes it has, but there are still many groups in society that have not been mentioned in the guidance that pose a threat to vulnerable children. There is no mention in the guidance of extreme behaviour towards children who many adults believe to be possessed by the devil and the practice of spirit possession. The London Safeguarding Children Board 2016 explains this form of abuse:

> A belief in spirit possession is not confined to particular countries, cultures, religions or communities. Common factors that put a child at risk of harm include: Belief in evil spirits: this is commonly accompanied by a belief that the child could 'infect' others with such 'evil'. The explanation for how a child becomes possessed varies widely, but includes through food that they have been given or through spirits that have flown around them.
>
> (London Safeguarding Children Board 2016)

In extreme cases children who are 'disobedient' or 'different' are believed to be possessed by a spirit controlling their behaviour. The children can be physically and emotionally abused to exorcise the spirit.

The Prevent duty guidance may also need to place more emphasis on the fact that a child is still a child until they turn 18 years. The recent uncovering of the sexual exploitation case in Rotherham found that the children involved were not recognised as children because of their age and were not deemed innocent initially because of their background (O'Caroll 2016). These children were sexually exploited and felt scared to come forward to relay their ordeals. Extreme behaviour has a negative effect on children; it does not protect them from harm.

NGO reports in Northern Ireland have serious concerns regarding young children being drawn into extreme groups that encourage violence as an induction into a group.

Just like legislation and guidance before the Security Act 2015, the Prevent duty guidance will need constant reflection and updating if we are truly to keep the safety and care of children at the forefront of our practice. Extreme groups may change depending on the climate of the times and so practitioners must be aware of the general terms that draw children from a young age in to extreme behaviour. Practitioners also need to be alert to signs that vulnerable children project if they are susceptible to extremism.

There is mainly a feeling of isolation and rejection from the groups they want to form positive attachments with, or anger and resentment because of information they have learnt that again isolates these children.

Understanding the Prevent duty guidance for Early Years practitioners

'The purpose must be to protect children from harm and to ensure that they are taught in a way that is consistent with the law and values' (HM Government 2011:69).

Practitioners working with the Early Years age range are at the forefront of contact with families and may see or hear things that do pose a threat to individuals.

The Prevent duty guidance has a two-pronged mission statement. First, children need to feel safe and recent safeguarding issues have extended this to issues such as radicalisation and extremism. Second, children need to have an inclusive environment in which to grow; they need to be nurtured by adults that believe in the values and ethos of that environment. Children do not feel safe when faced with extreme views, violence and exploitation. Practitioners need to be alert and knowledgeable about all extreme groups that follow such a negative way of life. There is an urgent need to put the safety of children first as the welfare of the child is paramount (The Children Act 1989).

> The success of Prevent work relies on communities supporting efforts to prevent people being drawn into terrorism and challenging the extremist ideas that are also part of terrorist ideology.
>
> (Prevent duty guidance 2015: 12, Point 144)

The role of the Early Years worker in implementing the Prevent duty guidance

Early Years providers serve arguably the most vulnerable and impressionable members of society. The Early Years Foundation Stage (EYFS) accordingly places clear duties on providers to keep children safe and promote their welfare. It makes clear that to protect children in their care, providers must be alert to any safeguarding and child protection issues in the child's life at home or elsewhere (DfE 2014b, paragraph 3.4).

> **Early Years providers must act to protect children from harm and should be alert to harmful behaviour by other adults in the child's life.**
>
> (HM Government 2015a: 7, Point 60)

Preventing by intervening

It is important to acknowledge why some children are vulnerable to extreme groups. They may feel isolated and not included in the communities where they live. They may have formed poor attachments and so are seeking any form of attachment that shows them attention. It is also possible that children may feel they are not listened to and feel angry and frustrated because they cannot voice opinions.

The way to deal with extreme views is to have intervention programmes in place so that there is a way out, and there is an understanding that someone will listen and protect. Hopefully this will stop and intercept these extremist views before they succeed in their negativity. When reflecting on the Prevent duty guidance, practitioners need to do so in a realistic and balanced way. They need to know what to do if they have a concern and how they can support children who feel so alienated that they may be at risk of this extremism. Early Years settings have a clear duty to build up positive relationships with families in the setting and provide opportunities for parents to work together and with the setting.

Practitioners also need to be clear about the procedure if there is a concern.

> where there is a concern for a child's welfare, this should be referred to local authority children's social care and if there is a reason to suspect a crime has been committed, the police should be involved.
>
> (DfE 2015a: 11)

Unlawful practices

There is also a need to know what practices are unlawful in this country such as FGM (female genital mutilation) forced marriages, and honour killings. Some practices such as FGM, which may be considered part of a ritual process for children, are not allowed in Britain and settings need to make sure cultures that practise this ritual understand it is not acceptable in Britain. The NSPCC has raised concerns that girls are being subjected to FGM at a younger age because parents are becoming wise to the fact that teachers are now more aware of the issue. In the UK, FGM is illegal. It is also illegal to take a British national or permanent resident abroad for FGM or to help someone trying to do this.

Signs that a child may have been subjected to FGM include being introverted, not attending nursery for a length of time, and presenting with sudden flu-like symptoms, which could be due to an infection. Other signs to look out for are if a child has returned from holiday and is complaining of tummy ache or hesitant about going to the toilet.

'If a teacher during their work in the profession discovers that an act of FGM appears to have been carried out on a girl under the age of 18 years old, it must be reported to the police' (DfE 2016, point 27 'keeping children safe'). The practice is now filtering to younger children and so all practitioners need to be vigilant. Cultures that practise customs that are not in line with British values are a cause for concern and may be defined as displaying traits of extremism.

Attendance recorded and monitored

There is a need to be alert to missing children and the worry of child abductions. Children that are missing education are of significant risk of underachieving, being victims of harm, exploitation and risk of radicalisation.

It is extremely important at this point to emphasise that radicalisation and extremism should not be directed at one group or one religion. It should be and needs to be stressed that it is extreme behaviour in whatever disguise.

The NSPCC has addressed some points to consider that have stemmed from serious case reviews: practitioners need to be aware that families who have English as an additional language need positive strategies in place in the setting to ensure that the parent or child is listened to. One parent may speak English and yet, if that family member is the abuser and the interpreter for the family, they may hide information and not interpret correctly

Other parents used as interpreters or children used as interpreter for families may not know the full picture or parents may not wish to share their concerns as they do not wish other parents to know their private business or children to be privy to such information. Settings need to understand that they make parents who do not speak English well aware that there are interpreters available if they need to voice concerns and they need to know that they can trust these interpreters and practitioners (NSPCC 2014a).

The Channel guidance

The Channel guidance gives advice on how to recognise and assess if there is a suspicion that a child may be open to radicalisation and extremism (HM Government 2012). Staff need to know what measures are available to prevent children from becoming drawn into terrorism and how to challenge the extremist ideology that can be associated with it. They need to understand how to obtain support for people who may be being exploited by radicalising influences. This has led to some boroughs being identified as areas that may be at risk

Prevent priority areas

Some areas of the UK have been defined as priority areas, namely some London boroughs and the most vulnerable areas of the United Kingdom. The Home Office will continue to identify priority areas for Prevent-related activity. Priority areas will, as now, be funded to employ a local Prevent co-ordinator to give additional support and expertise and additional Home Office grant funding is available for Prevent projects and activities. The Home Office will continue to have oversight of local Prevent co-ordinators and the funding, evaluation and monitoring of these projects.

Does this lull us in to a sense that it does not happen in areas that are not a priority?

In the same way that teachers are vigilant about signs of possible physical or emotional abuse in any of their pupils, if there is a concern for the safety of a specific young person at risk of radicalisation, the practitioner has a duty to follow safeguarding procedures, including discussing with your school's designated safeguarding lead the next steps.

When you read this as a teacher or practitioner, it may scare you and make you feel anxious. It raises questions as to what danger children in our care may be in and we can never ignore or dismiss any danger or concern of abuse as political scaremongering. This may lead us to wrongly assume that the guidance only refers to older children.

It may also have another effect on you as a practitioner. Many practitioners feel they do not know the best way to be alert and understanding regarding this issue. They may feel that they will cause offence and so may not pass on information or voice their concerns.

It is unclear as to what situations cause urgency or referral and what situations may need monitoring.

Good practice in the Early Years to keep children safe

It is important to communicate with parents about concerns that need to be addressed and this now extends to concerns regarding threats of radicalisation and exploitation. It is not easy to do. The most important consideration is to know your parents well and build trusting relationships with them. Examples of how to address issues under the Prevent duty are listed below:

- Know the British values and the laws of society well. Keep up to date with legislation and know the procedures to follow if there is a concern. This means that practitioners need to know what behaviours are contrary to British laws and be confident to challenge such behaviours.

- Settings need to display the British values, making it apparent what is acceptable and unacceptable. Making parents are aware of British values and the practices that are unlawful. Some settings have offered workshops, while others have displayed posters showing where support can be found.

- Practitioners need to be approachable to young children and their families and have safe places to talk if parents or children wish to confide in them.

- Good practice also needs practitioners to support children in developing a good self-esteem about themselves and a respect and care for others.

- Practitioners need to address confrontational vocabulary or negative attitudes displayed by parents or carers. Reminders to parents and carers need to be given and the message of what is said and how it is said in front of young children needs to be addressed.

- Settings need to support children from a young age to tell right from wrong. It is important that children form good secure attachments form an early age so that they learn that others care and in turn they will learn skills to care.

  A young child's experience of good attachments give him a sense of worth, a belief in the helpfulness of others and a favourable model on which to build future relationships.

  (Bowlby 1969: 378)

Once children feel safe and reassured in an inclusive environment, they will develop values and opinions of tolerance and respect.

Caring and supporting the practitioner

Practitioners need support when tackling any safeguarding issues, and the threat of extremism is a form of abuse. Many practitioners feel they will cause offence and may not pass on information or voice their concerns. They feel it is unclear as to what situations cause urgency or referral and what situations may need monitoring. Training and communication on a multi-agency level needs to be encouraged so that practitioners do not feel isolated or bear the responsibility on their own.

Many boroughs have clear procedures to follow if there is a concern and break down the types of concerns. For example, the London borough of Merton explains clearly what action needs to be taken if there is a concern.

> Any professional who identifies such concerns, for example, because of observed behaviour or reports of conversations to suggest the child/young person supports terrorism and/or extremism, must report these concerns to the named or designated safeguarding professional in their organisation or agency.
>
> Professionals should exercise professional judgement and common sense to identify whether an emergency situation applies. Examples in relation to extremism are expected to be very rare but would apply when there is information that a violent act is imminent, or where weapons or other materials may be in the possession of a young person, another member of their family or within the community. In this situation, a 999 call should be made.
>
> (Merton Safeguarding Children's Board n.d.)

Ultimately, practitioners need to follow the same procedures in place for safeguarding issues, but if there is a real threat that a violent act is imminent then the police need to be informed.

It is essential to realise that young people do not form extreme opinions overnight. It is because they have somehow felt isolated or rejected or have a low self-esteem or any of the other factors mentioned in this chapter, that leads them to a feeling of desperation to be included somewhere, even if the ideals are negative and threatening to others.

It is the responsibility of all the adults who care for children to instil in them from an early age a positive attitude and self-belief and a care for each other.

Practitioners need to refer to the theory of childhood attachment to gain an insight into self-image. 'Self-image' is the key to human personality and human behaviour. Change the self-image and you change the personality and the behaviour (Maltz n.d.).

Links to theory

Children from a very early age need a positive environment to grow and develop into adults that advocate goodness and care for our community and society. The work of

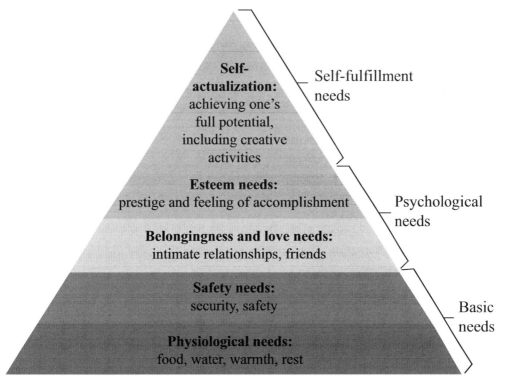

Figure 4.1 Every person is capable and has the desire to move up the hierarchy toward a level of self-actualization.

Abraham Maslow and Carl Rogers' research into children's needs commented on how to effectively support children to form a good self-esteem, self-worth and be positive in their outlook.

The first four levels of the five-stage model are often referred to as deficiency needs and are said to motivate people when they are unmet. For example, the longer a person goes without food the hungrier they will become. In the same way, the longer a child has a feeling of isolation or feels that they do not belong, the more he or she will not feel part of a group or community. Sadly, when this happens, children turn to other groups that instil fear or intimidation for them to belong. Gang culture often preys on young children who feel isolated. Extreme groups also coax children into a false sense of belonging and pride in the violence witnessed.

Carl Rogers, a psychologist, agreed with Maslow but added that the environment needed to be one of acceptance, empathy and needed to be genuine. He genuinely believed people are good and identified five characteristics of the fully functioning person:

1 **Open to experience**: both positive and negative emotions accepted. Negative feelings are not denied, but worked through. There is a place here for individual liberty freedom to express views and opinions but in a way, that is not antagonistic or threatening to others.

2 **Existential living**: in touch with different experiences as they occur in life, avoiding prejudging and preconceptions. Being able to live and fully appreciate the present, not always looking back to the past or forward to the future. The sense of rejection and isolation that many communities felt in the past should not have a direct impact on the here and now. Lessons have been learnt but times should have changed and moved on.

3 **Trust feelings**: feeling, instincts and gut-reactions are paid attention to and trusted. People's own decisions are the right ones and we should trust ourselves to make the right choices.

4 **Creativity**: creative thinking and risk taking are features of a person's life. A person does not play safe all the time. This involves the ability to adjust and change and seek new experiences.

5 **Fulfilled life**: person is happy and satisfied with life, and always looking for new challenges and experiences.

Rogers (1959) believed that the closer our self-image and ideal-self are to each other, the higher our sense of self-worth.

If children from a young age do not develop a good self-esteem or do not feel a sense of belonging and form good secure attachments, the negativity that they experience will develop into a negative attitude of themselves and of others and often specific groups.

Preventing this from happening should be the main aim of the practitioner and the main purpose of the Prevent duty guidance.

Putting it into practice

Practitioners need clear duties on how to keep children safe and promote their welfare.

- Children that are vulnerable to extremism are susceptible to a form of abuse. Staff need to think of the signs of this abuse and be alert to changes in behaviour, inappropriate language or actions. Practitioners need to have a clear understanding of signs children may show if they are open to extreme behaviours. Children may comment or use inappropriate derogatory language heard on television programmes or within their families or communities that needs to be addressed.

- Practitioners need to know what to do if they have a concern and how they can support children who feel so alienated that they may be at risk of this extremism. They need to follow the correct procedures and be honest and objective in their responses.

- Children may suddenly not attend settings with no reason given for their absence. They may return withdrawn or angry. Monitoring attendance is vital for the welfare of the child.

- Training needs to include how to deal with sensitive issues and how it needs to be approached sensitively and objectively. Practitioners do not want to alienate parents and risk further isolating parents that may feel unwelcome or not part of a community. Our role is to keep children safe and promote their welfare. It makes clear that to protect children in their care, providers must be alert to any safeguarding and child protection issues in the child's life at home or elsewhere (DfE 2014b, paragraph 3.4).

- Robust safeguarding policies should include a clear understanding of the risk to children of radicalisation. There is a need to have a named safeguarding lead and safeguarding arrangements need to be in line with local safeguarding boards (LSCBs).

- There needs to be in place safe recruitment processes so that settings monitor sufficiently those staff who apply and work with children are promoting positive relationships.

- A safe visitors' policy needs to highlight to visitors and speakers the setting, the ethos of the setting and the policies and procedures that they need to adhere to.

- Interventions are projects intended to divert people who are being drawn into terrorist activity. Interventions can include mentoring, counselling, theological support, encouraging civic engagement, developing support networks (family and peer structures) or providing mainstream services (education, employment, health, finance or housing).

- Settings need to provide a safe learning environment with focused activities and routines. Settings need to encourage activities that enable children to learn to negotiate and take turns from a young age. They need to promote activities that help children learn how to remain calm and give them skills in how to express opinions in a clear but non-judgemental way. For example, activities such as yoga, mindfulness and persona dolls could create a calm environment and a platform for children to express opinions in a non-confrontational way. Practitioners need to know their children, have a key person system in place but also come together to share information about key children.

- Where applicable, professionals should record the ethnicity, culture and faith of families that they work with. This information should be shared across agencies. The implications that ethnicity, culture and faith might have on family relationships should be considered. Professionals need the confidence to challenge parents who raise matters of race or religion to distract attention from a focus on the child (NSPCC 2014b).

- When we consider extremism, it is important to listen to the language of children in their role play and one area that needs addressing particularly with our young children is age appropriate computer games and TV programmes. If a child started to talk about an inappropriate television programme that they had been watching, or a computer game that encourages violence, practitioners need to feel confident to address this issue with parents.

- Extremism does not just appear in a child's life. It is when children are faced with images, opinions, language and actions that are extremely violent or negative from an early age that they then use these images to make a distorted sense of their world. It may be a slow process that needs monitoring or sharing with other agencies. If experiences, images and language are positive, children will be less susceptible to violent or erratic behaviour that they could see and grow up thinking is the norm.

There is a need to constantly reflect on practice by asking some very important questions.

- 'Does the setting and especially the manager understand how children are at risk of being exposed to extreme ideas about right and wrong?

- Have staff completed specialist training to make sure they understand how to support vulnerable families?

- What activities and experiences does a setting promote to encourage and support children from an early age to understand compromise, negotiation, sharing and remaining calm?

Summary

Fear of the unknown is often the worst type of fear. It makes a community anxious and exaggerates fear factors. The Prevent duty guidance should not be a guidance that causes division and provokes certain groups, isolating them. It is a guidance that calls on those services working with children to realise their duty of care is for the child first and foremost. It possibly needs to go deeper in identifying the many extreme groups that could be a threat to children; the NSPCC has started to identify such groups from serious case reviews. Non-government organisations have also identified children that are a concern and vulnerable to extremism.

It is a document that asks settings to have robust safeguarding procedures in place and practitioners need to be aware of signs that may be portrayed by young people that are vulnerable to extremism and radicalisation. Above all, the Prevent duty guidance offers ways to prevent this type of abuse through offering intervention programmes and building up positive relationships within the community. This goes hand in hand with encouraging our nation to have mutual respect and tolerance. Thus, having an impact on our curriculum for the youngest children in our community.

Fostering a sense of belonging
Valuing the unique child and supporting positive relationships

There are four themes that run through the Early Years Foundation Stage curriculum (EYFS) that should be integral to daily practice:

Table 5.1 Four themes of the Early Years Foundation Stage curriculum

The unique child	Positive relationship	Enabling environment	Learning and development
Every child is a unique child who is constantly learning and can be resilient, capable, confident and self-assured (DfE 2014b: 6)	Children learn to be strong and independent through positive relationships. (DfE 2014b: 6)	Children learn and develop well in enabling environments (DfE 2014b: 6)	Children learn and develop in different ways and at different rates (DfE 2014b: 6)

The next two chapters focus on these themes and gives examples of how they promote British values effectively in practice.

The EYFS theme 1: the unique child

Every child is a unique child who is constantly learning and can be resilient, capable, confident and self-assured.

(DfE 2014b: 6)

The practitioner's role in the Early Years setting is to support children growing into independent thinkers and to encourage them to have a positive self-worth and clear sense of belonging. Practitioners support children in making choices and decisions but also help them to gain a responsibility that they are part of a community and so need to be sensitive of their opinions, portraying them in a positive, respectful way.

Figure 5.1 Every child is a unique child who is constantly learning and can be resilient, capable and confident.

Links with British values

By respecting the needs and interests of the individual child and acknowledging that each child is unique, practitioners are creating the idea that children have the freedom to make choices and voice opinion. This is the essence of individual liberty. Accepting identity and celebrating differences, but at the same time understanding national identity and accepting what they have in common will reassure children and make them feel secure that they belong. It will help them make sense of the wider world. When practitioners have a clear definition of identity and a sense of belonging, they form an understanding of how to impart this to children in their care. That is why it is important to reflect on the definition of British values and understand identity so that settings can effectively promote and celebrate this in a significant way.

Every child is different. Children develop at different rates and need different kinds of support. Children also need to gain skills that enable them to be resilient, confident individuals and grow to become responsible members of a community and society.

How can this be achieved?

The unique child reaches out to relate to people and things through the characteristics of effective learning.

(DfE 2014b: 6)

Practitioners can support the decisions that children make and provide activities that involve turn-taking, sharing and collaboration. Children should be given opportunities to develop enquiring minds in an atmosphere where questions are valued. Practitioners can also ensure that children understand their own and others' behaviour and its consequences, learning to distinguish right from wrong in a safe and secure environment.

Children should develop a positive sense of themselves. Practitioners can provide opportunities for children to develop their self-knowledge, self-esteem and increase their confidence in their own abilities. For example, managing risks enables children to grow in their confidence and independence and, through allowing children to take risks, they begin to know their capabilities and grow in resilience.

Practitioners should encourage a range of experiences that allow children to explore the language of feelings and responsibility, reflect on their differences and accept that they are free to have different opinions but not to the detriment of being abusive and aggressive towards others. This is an important message for adults to also accept.

Every Child Matters (2003) is one of the main documents that acknowledges the unique child. From an early age, children need to know that they belong, they need to feel safe and reassured that they can enjoy and take risks in their play to become 'capable and resilient' (DfE 2014b: 6) in their development.

The key factor in creating a sense of belonging for the unique child is to support children from an early age in how to develop a positive sense of their own identity and culture, affirming that every child is unique and needs to be loved and cared for so that they grow up confident in proclaiming their identity. Opportunities for active learning, play and exploring, creating and thinking critically, enable children to take ownership of their play. These characteristics enable children from an early age to have a go and learn to manage risks effectively, building up their resilience and confidence. Practitioners need to praise them for persevering, concentrating, having their own ideas, choosing ways to do thing and solving problems.

Links to theories

Goleman described this resilience as 'emotional self-management' (2006: 166) In building up their resilience, children gain strength to deal with situations and, as they grow older and feel confident, responses to difficult situations may be easier to deal with. If the rules are understood and agreed from an early age, children will also understand the difference between right and wrong and will be confident in following rules that ultimately keep them safe. This may mean keeping themselves safe from bullying but also from extremism and negative attitudes that lead to radicalisation.

> If we want to form men and women, nothing will fit in so well for the task as to study the laws that govern their formation.
>
> (Piaget 1965: 413)

If the laws are fair, consistent, learnt and agreed from an early age, children will have formed a sense of right and wrong, fair and unfair. They will be ready to be responsible for their actions and hopefully have the skills to speak out against the negative or extreme actions of others.

Children need to learn boundaries. They feel safe and secure within boundaries and eager to explore. However, boundaries should not suffocate their development. For this growth to be successful, children need to form attachments with adults that are caring and supportive from an early age. Children also need to have positive role models throughout their lives as most rules that a child learns are learnt from adults and peers that are influential in their lives.

Forming their own identity is crucial to children's growth into independent self-assured adults. It is imperative that there is an understanding and acceptance of the identities of others and encouraging them to feeling part of a shared common identity. This is the essence of British values in practice and can be achieved right from birth. Opportunities for babies to have meaningful contact with familiar adults through engagement such as gestures, eye contact and laughing will build up their confidence and self-esteem. Children learn as they get older to resolve conflict, to initiate conversations and listen to others in a polite way. The unique child is observed by the practitioner to ensure that they are respected and 'have access to Early Years provision that fosters their unique aptitudes and abilities and enables them to thrive and develop' (Sargent 2016: 10). Every child should have access to Early Years provision that respects their uniqueness enabling them to thrive and develop.

Planning

Planning needs to consider the interests, needs and abilities of each child and must be inclusive in its approach. In practice, this is carried out through the Early Years Foundation Stage curriculum. The curriculum is made up of **three prime areas:**

- Personal, social and emotional development (PSED)
- Communication and language development (CLL)
- Physical development (PD)

These are the main areas to focus on from birth to 3 years old.

And four specific areas:

- Literacy (L)
- Mathematical development (MD)
- Understanding the world (UTW)
- Expressive art and design (EAD)

Early Years settings need to take time and practitioners need to value the small steps that are involved in the process of identity in young children. For example, encouraging children to help to tidy up and take care of their environment, leads to responsibility and a sense of ownership in their community.

The concepts and learning involved in play is far deeper than first observed. A simple task such as helping to tidy up sends out so many messages of working together and ultimately lays the foundations for British values in practice. When practitioners support children in the smallest of tasks and experiences, they are beginning to understand the real message of British values. Children need time to explore, to make sense of their world and the world around them, to communicate with others and to learn the rules of communication, to learn what is meant by fairness and equality through sharing and

Table 5.2 Links to the EYFS – the unique child

Age	The unique child self-confidence and self-awareness	Making relationships
0–20 months	Contacts people by laughing, gestures, voice and eye contact	Recognises and responsive to main carers voice
	Engages with other person to achieve goals such as getting an object out of reach	Responds to carer
		Likes cuddles and being held
16–30 months	Demonstrates sense of self as an individual wants to do things independently	Plays cooperatively
		Plays alongside others
22–36 months	Separates from main carer	Shows affection and concern for people who are special to them
	Expresses own preferences and interests	
30–50 months	Enjoys responsibility of carrying out small tasks	Demonstrates friendly behaviour initiating conversations and forming good relationships with peers and familiar adults
	Shows confidence in asking for help	
	Confident in talking to others freely about home and community	
40–60months	Can describe self in positive terms and talk about their abilities	Takes steps to resolve conflicts with others by finding a compromise or negotiating
	Confident to speak to others about own needs, wants, interests and opinions	Initiates conversations and takes account of what others say

Note: Adapted from DfE (2014b) Early Years Foundation Stage curriculum guidance learning goals.

Figure 5.2 Enjoys responsibility of carrying out small tasks.

turn taking and negotiating and compromise. And this can be apparent in the small daily tasks and experiences that they have opportunities to be part of in the Early Years setting such as tidy up time, preparing snacks, playing games with each other, caring for each other and time for them to be themselves, learning to express themselves in an appropriate and positive way. It is also evident in how practitioners respond to children. If routines such as snack time or tidy up time are rushed, the opportunity for learning is lost and often it is through routines and daily activities that children gain the skills to develop personally, socially and emotionally. In the Early Years Foundation Stage curriculum, Kathy Brodie describes the areas of personal social and emotional development as 'the bedrock of learning' (Brodie 2014: 39), which needs to be supported by 'sensitive and caring adults' (Brodie 2014: 39).

The unique child should be visible throughout the Early Years. And the unique child, playing and interacting with others, is the foundation for British values in practice.

Figure 5.3 Children should enjoy learning about a range of cultures so they grow up understanding difference instead of fearing it. They need opportunities to engage in activities and experiences that help them to share and take turns.

For children to move on from their learning they also need to be able to work and play cooperatively and collaboratively.

(Sargent 2016: 14)

The Early Years setting provides an environment where children can learn to be themselves but also play with others, engaging in activities and experiences that help them to share, negotiate, take turns and compromise.

Finally, the unique child cannot learn in isolation. For the unique child to thrive in the Early Years setting, they need positive relationships with their peer group and adults.

The EYFS theme 2: positive relationships

Children learn to be strong and independent through positive relationships.

(DfE 2014b: 6)

In Britain, Early Years settings include childminders, private nurseries, pre-schools and state nurseries and children's centres. All settings have the responsibility to promote opportunities for the unique child to thrive and develop. These values should be inherent in all societies over the world but it is important to focus on Britain. Learning is often limited to maths, literacy and science but real learning and development needs a firm foundation in personal, social and emotional development for children to have a clear understanding and accept the British values of rule of law, individual liberty, democracy and mutual respect and tolerance.

Links with British values

By fostering positive relationships with parents, practitioners and other professionals, and by treating everyone fairly and understanding that children have the right to participate (UNCRC 2015, Article 12), practitioners are sowing the seeds for democracy. The role of the practitioner is to promote positive values and tolerance in the education of children. British values give practitioners a foundation to know how to form good attachments with children in their care. They link well with the theory of child development.

Links to theory

Albert Bandura, a behaviourist theorist, believed children imitate their caregivers and peers to understand the world that they live in (Lindon 2005). Therefore, as practitioners, we play a vital role in how children grow up to become responsible adults as they take their cue from the adults around them. As Jerome Bruner summarised in his work, the role of the adult is first and foremost one of the most influential factors in children's development at a young age (Lindon 2005). Because of this, as a society, there is a need for a set of values that are followed and adhered to. British values in practice are defining a moral code that we, as adults need to adhere to, as well as supporting children, thus recognising these values as a foundation for being a responsible member of society.

Lawrence Kohlberg (1927–1987) based much of his work on the theories of Jean Piaget's studies on the cognitive development of children and is best known for his work on moral development. He explains that there are three levels of moral development:

- Level 1 — pre-conventional: children's decisions are based on avoiding punishment and receiving rewards
- Level 2 — convention: upholding the rules of society
- Level 3 — post-conventional: individuals follow universal moral principles that may be more important to a group or country (Crain 1985: 118).

Communities need rules to follow that are relevant for the place that they live in. It is the responsibility of the practitioners, professionals and parents that work and care for children to support them in growing strong and independent. They need good role models to see how this can be successful and positive relationships from birth to feel secure in their growth and development. Ensuring that the beginning of a young child's life is rooted in love, care, respect and discipline is vital. It is the responsibility of adults who care for children to give each child a chance to flourish and grow in to a positive member of a community. The attachment theories of John Bowlby, Harry Harlow and Mary Ainsworth focus on children having good attachments in life for them to feel good about themselves.

Response to theory

By understanding the theory of attachment, practitioners are enabled to understand their role as an attachment figure. John Bowlby realised that children need secure attachments from a caregiver, initially their mother, but later he realised it could be a main carer, and this was vital to a child's growth and development. Good attachments ensure that children form good relationships later in life. The work of Perry Szalavitz described by Brodie (2014: 40) explains that 'poor attachments and lack of emotional bonding affects the development of the brain'. This emphasises how vital it is for children, from an early age, to have good positive attachments in their lives from the start. Practitioners are one of the key persons in a child's life. Response to their behaviour, their personality and their development has a huge impact on their growth and self-esteem. Practitioners play an enormous role in a child's life ensuring the beginning of a young child's life is rooted in love, care, respect and discipline. For this reason, when examining British values in practice, adults must follow the rules and code outlined by our society. Practitioners, just like parents, will have an influence on children's lives.

It takes a society to nurture a child successfully. The work of Urie Bronfenbrenner summarised the influences on a child's life. He argued that 'to understand human development, one must consider the entire ecological system in which growth occurs' (Bronfenbrenner 1979: 6) and explained the whole system as divided in to subsystems.

1 Microsystem – in this system are the child's immediate family and surroundings are influential to the child's development. Having positive family attachments helps the child to form positive attachments and a good self-image and self-worth.

2 Mesosystem – the broader surroundings and influences on the child's development. This system includes the pre-school, doctors' surgery and other influences on the child's and family's life. This shows that the community in which a child lives in needs to be a community that he or she also feels part of.

3 Exosystem – a broader circle of people who indirectly influence the child. Things in the exosystem include the parent's workplace, the services available to the family and the support networks they are involved in.

4 Macrosystem – this is an even broader system that includes the values, customs and attitudes of the cultural group the child belongs to. This is important as it also enables us to understand why the practitioner needs to foster a sense of belonging and why identity is so important.

Bronfenbrenner explains that the interaction between parents and practitioners also influences a child. Partnership with parents is vital in Early Years practice; positive relationships need to be formed with all parents and carers to achieve the best development for children. A democratic environment is one where all parents and children are included and involved in the learning process.

> There is an expectation that all children and their families will be respected and valued and not discriminated against on any basis.
>
> (Sargent 2016: 10)

Early Years settings need to reflect the needs of the community. They need to have things in place that welcome families to the setting; they need to be approachable and give time to parents.

For example, parents who may not have English as their first language may need access to interpreters or communication strategies that support them in their understanding information. Parents who may work long hours and cannot attend parents' consultations during the day may need opportunities for convenient times to meet with the manager and key person to discuss the learning of their child. Some parents may have had negative experiences of school when they were growing up and so may need time and opportunities to see the positive environment their child now attends to feel welcome and reassured to approach members of staff.

However, it must be added that for British values in practice to be effective, parenting skills also need to be addressed. Poor parenting needs to be identified and supported. British values go beyond the needs of the child and extend a warm and welcoming hand to all parents and carers. British values need to be explained to parents so that they are not misinterpreted and do not have a negative impact on children. Partnership with parents needs to include explaining to parents that need support how they can support their child at home in making good responsible choices, understanding right from wrong, realising appropriate forms of communication and not using inappropriate language that could be copied by their child.

Children will form many attachments in their lives. Positive attachments come from many sources and as children get older, these sources include the media, the community and their peers as well as practitioners and families. Therefore, the whole of society need to be built on the same foundations. There is a need for British values within our society at this present moment if positive relationships are to be successful. All Early Years settings need to ensure that British values are at the heart of a child's holistic

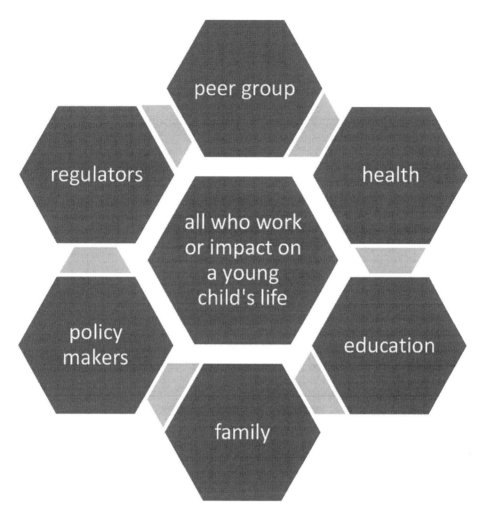

Figure 5.4 All those who work or impact on a young child's life.

development and that they develop a positive understanding of their community and the wider world in which they live.

The role of the adult is simply to listen and respond, to lay good secure foundations to help children thrive and achieve, to get to know the children in their care and ensure the child has smooth transitions in their lives. The adult needs to be a good role model for this to be successfully achieved.

Links with the EYFS and British values

By listening and responding to children from birth, practitioners are listening to their responses, understanding their likes and interests. This is the beginning of participation, allowing them as they get older to be involved in the decision-making processes of the setting. Good practice 'starts from the child' (Sargent 2016: 17) but it does not end with the child. Good practice needs to extend to parents and carers and needs to create an inclusive environment where parents feel reassured by the child's workforce. Teaching children the importance of caring for each other, taking responsibility for their actions, understanding consequences of their actions and involving them in decisions is the responsibility of all the adults that are forming positive relationships with the children in their care.

Table 5.3 Positive relationships links to the EYFS

Area of learning

PSED making relationships

Age/development	Role of practitioner	British values in practice
Birth–20 months		
Reacts emotionally to other people's emotions and shows a range of emotions Calms when being upset when held or cuddle or rocked, spoken or sung to in a soothing voice	Listen to the child in their care. Respond to them Be a good role model Find out as much as you can from parents Learn lullabies that children know from home Suggest to parents that they bring in a comforter from home	When following law, children and adults need to understand the rules, which requires good listening and attention skills. From birth, as a practitioner, we are saying, I will hold you when you cry and comfort you. I will make sure you feel calm and reassured.
16–36 months		
Plays alongside others and plays cooperatively with a familiar adult Shows affection and concern for people who are special to them	Include all children in welcoming and caring for each other Help children to understand the feelings of others by labelling emotions Help them to understand the rules for being together with others Model ways of noticing how others are feeling	By supporting children how to play together, we are laying the foundations for them to understand the importance of turn taking and sharing and modelling fair treatment, which is the essence of democracy that everyone should be treated fairly

Area of learning

PSED making relationships

Age/development	Role of practitioner	British values in practice
30–60 months		
Initiates play, demonstrates friendly behaviour, forming good relationships with peers and familiar adults	Challenge negative comments and actions towards peers or adults Help children to understand the feelings of others Plan support for children who have not yet made friends	Teaching children there are consequences to negative actions from an early age enable children to understand rules and acceptable behaviour Also, teaching them to care for each other and have empathy enables them to grow up with a respect for others Democracy also lends itself to enabling children to take responsibility and share responsibility, working together to form positive relationships
40–60 months		
Takes steps to resolve conflicts, for example, finding a compromise	Model being considerate and responsive in interactions Ensure there are opportunities to listen to each other Be aware of and respond to the needs of children who are learning English as an additional language Talk about how they are feeling Talk about their own behaviour and others' behaviour and its consequences and know that some behaviour is unacceptable	Children need to learn from an early age what makes appropriate behaviour and what happens if rules are broken and the consequences. Routines will help and support children to know what is expected of them.

Note: Adapted from DfE (2014b) Early Years Foundation Stage curriculum.

A quality workforce is vital

When children feel cared for and respected and when their parents can see a quality workforce, outcomes can improve. The Nutbrown Review (June 2012) emphasised the need for a good quality workforce to be in place where practitioners had a deep understanding of child development.

> High quality early education and childcare can have a positive long term impact on children's later learning and achievements.
>
> (Nutbrown Review, June 2012)

British values in practice

If the unique child is at the forefront of practice and if positive relationships are fostered, settings need to have policies, procedures and practices in place that respect the individual child recognising their needs, interests and abilities. It also needs to have a rigorous system in place where practitioners are recruited for their expertise and professionalism as well as having qualities such as care, respect, and being a good role model for the children they are there to support.

> Children learn not only from what we intend to teach but from all their experiences.
>
> (Pugh and Duffy 2014: 188)

The ethos of a setting is paramount to successful early learning. Children learn from each other, from practitioners and from parents' values and how to respect and care for others.

> To create a positive ethos for practice, staff in every setting will need to explore what the ethos in their setting feels like to the users, for example parents, children and staff.
>
> (Pugh and Duffy 2014: 189)

This starts well before children arrive at the setting. To foster a sense of belonging, settings need to have in place clear policies and procedures that ensure the workforce is skilled and suitable to work with children. To have this in place, settings are proclaiming that they value their workforce, they value their children and they want the best for the children in their care. Safe recruitment procedures, suitable skilled staff and the role of each member of staff ensure the workforce is motivated, committed and skilled at supporting children. This is something that happens up and down the country, in pre-schools, childminders homes, private day care and school settings.

The statutory requirements for the Early Years Foundation Stage states:

> Every child deserves the best possible start in life and support that enables them to fulfil their potential.
>
> (DfE 2014b: 5, Point 1)

The Early Years Foundation Stage is divided in to two sections. One section focuses on learning and development and one section focuses on safeguarding and welfare requirements. The welfare requirements highlight the importance of having suitable people looking after children.

> Providers must ensure that people looking after children are suitable to fulfil the requirements of their roles.
>
> (DfE 2014b, 3.9 EYFS statutory requirements)

This reassures parents and children, knowing that they are safe as they play and learn and they are receiving quality care.

British values in practice that links to positive relationships needs to include:

An ethos displayed

A setting should actively display its message of collaboration and uniqueness that proclaims this is the positive learning that is taking place here for children to be confident individuals but also responsible members of a community from an early age. The ethos needs to have the British values as the focus of its mission statement. The ethos is personal to the setting and relevant to the community but British values are central to its message.

Case study

The head teacher of Lilleshall Primary School in Shropshire, Christobel Cousins, explains how the school creates an ethos that promotes positive relationships and values the unique child.

> The school's mission statement is 'Working together for excellence and enjoyment' and this underpins everything we do. We aim to work together to ensure all pupils reach their full potential; however, we feel very strongly that children should enjoy their primary years. We aim to offer a curriculum that is engaging, exciting and will provide life long memories. The school promotes the key British values that

underpin our society and enable our pupils to value the things we have that may otherwise be taken for granted and their true worth not realised, such as democracy, the rule of law, mutual respect and tolerance. We recognise that as individuals we all have different experiences, views and opinions and these are what make us unique, what we need to do as a school is harness these and enable pupils to respect and value the opinions of others by understanding why they hold these views and the experiences that have influenced them. Enabling pupils with different religious beliefs to share how they celebrate their beliefs provides other pupils with a clear understanding of how that faith works in practice, it has certainly improved my knowledge and understanding. We also endeavour to ensure that we also consider the values of Christianity, which can be lost as we use Churches to perform Christmas productions and carol services but forget to teach the respect we should have for these places and the meaning of the signs and symbols held within them. We need balance and understanding. This way pupils feel valued and develop the knowledge to make choices.

A safe recruitment process

Settings that ensure their staff are suitable and have the skills and qualities to work with children achieve a workforce that is motivated and committed to good practice. Disclosure and Barring Service (DBS) checks, identity checks, references and CVs will all build up a picture of the staff that are employed. Safe recruitment also responds to the Prevent duty guidance. Ensuring that staff are suitable and identity checks made reassures parents that the setting is keeping children safe and informing regulatory bodies if they do not feel children are safe. Stringent requirements such as the disqualification requirements (DfE 2014b, 3.14 of the Statutory Framework) ensure robust systems are in place, thus keeping children safe.

A clear whistleblowing policy and procedure

Practitioners need to be confident in communicating with their line mangers if they are unhappy with the way that a child has been spoken to or handled. Managers need to consider how to make and enforce make the rules of the setting. They need to ask the questions regularly:

- How do we hear the voice of the child?
- How do we hear the voice of the parents?
- Are the rules of the setting known to all and where are they displayed?
- Do they ensure that staff use positive language and negative phrases are picked up on so that they do not continually occur?
- Do they take complaints seriously and keep a record of the complaint and how it has been resolved?

- Are staff aware of the routines and how they need to ensure that they are following the correct procedures, especially during personal care routines.

- How do staff ensure that they are alert to extreme behavior? Extreme behaviour, sadly, is not something new and it remains crucial that staff need to think the unthinkable at times.

(Rushworth 2010)

Highly qualified staff

Regarding CV writing, those applying for jobs with young children need to explain the qualities and skills that they possess that will help children in their care to learn and develop. For example, a member of staff may have a musical talent or speak another language. The employer may feel this would be an asset to their setting as they could take responsibility for music sessions or they may have parents who speak the same language and this could help them to access the setting easier. The Nutbrown Review (2012) felt that most staff in Early Years should be qualified to a certain standard and many managers now have furthered their education.

> Excellent pedagogical leadership is vital in improving the quality of provision, and all Early Years practitioners can aspire to be pedagogical leaders. Progression opportunities need to be accessible for all capable and committed women and men.
>
> (The Nutbrown Review: 2012: 7)

This gives a setting a clear understanding of child development, of new initiatives that show how children learn effectively. It keeps staff up to date with knowledge and they feel confident in supporting children. Working with children requires practitioners to have a passion about child development and learning.

Some appear to think that working with young children means nothing more than changing nappies and wiping noses. This is a misconception of what it is to work with young children and is an insult to young children. The Nutbrown Review highlighted practitioners' 'dismay at the lack of public understanding, or appreciation, of the work they do' (2012: 16).

Knowing the children in your care and their families

The role of the practitioner is also to get to know the children in their care. It is essential that practitioners know their children, know their likes and dislikes, and know their interests and specific needs. They should be able to identify their needs and interests, plan for their next steps and enjoy being with the children that they care for. Observation assessment and planning needs to 'broaden a child's experience to make a wider range of choices' (Sancisi and Edgington 2015: 25).

Play and learning enables children to make sense of the world and build up resilience if things don't go to plan. It also helps them to be flexible, make choices and decisions and know how and where to seek help. The role of the practitioner is to support children learning these skills, which are skills that equip them for the future. The practitioner also needs to know the family of the child, to feel confident sharing information and set up a communication flow to learn from each other. If a child feels loved and wanted, they immediately get a sense of belonging and so the key person system, settling in procedures and welcoming children into the setting are vital when fostering a sense of belonging.

A secure and reassuring key person system

A key person is 'someone who builds up a significant and special relationship with the child and their parents. This relationship is a close one and allows the child to cope and feel emotionally secure in the absence of their parents' (Tassoni 2014: 59).

The key person is a statutory requirement as we see it as vital in fostering a sense of belonging. Children need to feel comfortable staying with adults.

Vivian Gussin Paley, a theorist, advocates if practitioners just do one thing a day that should be to make sure that they speak to every child in their care (Paley 2008). The key person should not only work and interact with their children but get to know all the children in a setting. Arrangements need to be made to ensure that if the key person is not working on a day, then a buddy system is in place. All these practices help to make the child and the family feel reassured and safe and secure, which promotes a positive self-image, confidence and boosts self-esteem.

There are many ways a key person and adults in the setting can get to know children in their care, for example:

- Getting to know children through home visits
- Stay and play sessions
- Informal meetings with parents at the beginning and end of each day
- Sharing information about routines
- Shared observations. Home observations can be shared with the setting
- Finding out the ethnic group of the child and the customs and traditions that are prevalent in the family and building this in to planning
- Finding out about special people in the child's life such as grandparents, aunties and cousins
- The key person effectively is becoming part of the family when he or she takes the role of key person.

Encouraging children to form positive relationships with each other

Practitioners need to know when to stand back and allow children time to form positive relationships with each other.

> 'ELG 08' Making relationships: pupils play co-operatively, taking turns with others. They take account of one another's ideas about how to organise their activity. They show sensitivity to others' needs and feelings, and form positive relationships with adults and other.
>
> (DfE 2017)

Encouraging positive relationships amongst parents

Practitioners also need to foster positive relationships amongst parents. Having days where parents can meet often helps to foster a sense of belonging.

Many settings have Father's Day where dads come to stay and play or grandparents' days, where adults are invited in to the setting and stay and play with the children. It enables adults that are close to the child to spend some precious time with them in the environment of the setting.

Opportunities for mutual respect and tolerance can be supported by sharing and celebrating festivals and traditions together. For example, an international day that celebrates all the languages spoken in the setting or the variety of foods eaten can prove to be successful in getting parents to talk to each other. It also alerts practitioners to parents that may feel isolated and do not know how to form those initial friendships.

Systems need to be in place to show that settings do not tolerate abuse from parents or inappropriate language or opinions that are antagonistic and discriminatory. It is often the case that Early Years settings encourage and support parent partnership and positive relationships with parents but the contact diminishes when children enter primary and secondary school. Fostering a sense of belonging needs to be a continuous aim throughout a child's school.

One school in Shropshire, Lilleshall Primary School, explains how it fosters positive relationships with parents.

Conversation with the head teacher, Christobel Cousins, and head of RE, Maria Hogan

> Do parents feel part of a community and how? We endeavour to ensure that our parents feel part of the school community by firstly having an open-door policy where parents can request to see the head teacher at any time and if possible this will be accommodated, usually instantly. When talking to parents I always say that I would

like them to come to me with a small worry or concern rather than let it build into something bigger. This means parents feel supported and understood. I try to ensure that I am on the playground two or three mornings a week to chat with parents. Parents are also invited to induction meetings and term evaluations and progress meetings for reception children. All parents are invited to Parent Days in the autumn and spring term. Parents with pupils with special educational needs and disability (SEND) are invited to regular reviews and additional progress meetings. Usually in the autumn term there is an information evening for parents with a presentation and pupil workshops. These will focus on a key area of development within school and enable parents to support their children effectively at home. These evenings have focused on reading, mathematics and spelling so far. To ensure the school has a feeling of community we also organise other events that do raise money but for me the key purpose of these is the promotion of the school community; these include the Easter Bingo, Christmas Fair, Sports Week, Summer Fair and charity events. The school also offers an Early Intervention Worker for pupils and parents to support them when families or individuals are having a tricky time. This support makes sure that there is provision beyond the school gate and that families can quickly access support that will help make a difference. The head teacher provides support for parents with managing children's behaviour at home when families are finding this challenging. Parental surveys and questionnaires are used to help the school identify what it does well and what it could do better. We sometimes think we are doing something well and for all the right reasons but it is only the person on the receiving end who really knows how it works for them. I see the parents as our customers, education is not cheap and parents pay for it in their taxes and they deserve a quality service and our pupils deserve the best.

Provide smooth transitions

The role of the practitioner is to ensure the children have smooth transition in their lives and they support these transitions. The sense of belonging doesn't stop when a child leaves one setting for another. The impact of a bereavement or a change in a child's life, such as divorce or moving home, cannot be ignored. Practitioners need to think about the summary work they hand over at work so that the new practitioner gains an idea of what the child likes, struggles with or enjoys.

Being a good role model

Finally, the role of the adult is to be a good role model.

Practitioners must support children in their interactions with others by interacting positively with the children and families in their care. It is vital how the practitioner ensures that they welcome all families into the setting. They need to take time to talk to children and families at the beginning and end of the day. They need to be polite and courteous in their demeanour to families. They need to be confidential in their practice and ensure their personal life does not impact on their professional life. This requires that the practitioner is aware that he or she needs to remain professional always.

Social media accounts

Managers need to ensure that their staff are aware of the rules regarding confidentiality and that they know how to behave with each other. In fostering a sense of belonging we need to get along as a group; we need to share good practice and point out negative attitudes or poor communication.

The mobile phone policy should address such issues as turning off the phone whilst in the setting but also extends to being confidential when accessing social media such as Facebook and Twitter accounts.

Case study – Early Years setting: Parkside Pre-School

An example of a practice that promotes British values

The manager, Debbie Murphy, welcomes me in to the setting. Displayed in the entrance are many signs depicting the home languages of the children.

Debbie Murphy explains that they start with the child, the culture of the child, language of the children, dietary needs of the child and interests of the child. An ethnicity table records what is special to the child as many children may be from the same race or religion or culture but may celebrate in many ways.

Festivals and customs are celebrated by all, and parents are asked to come in to the setting and retell some traditional stories or take a group for a cooking activity around the tradition or festival.

Parents' wishes are respected all the time. For example, some parents who were Jehovah's Witnesses did not want their child to celebrate Christmas or birthdays. However, some parents who were Jehovah's Witnesses were happy for their children to take part in the celebrations. Debbie adds that it is important to respect parents' wishes. She adds that the celebration of different customs and traditions helps everyone in the setting to gain knowledge and an understanding of different faiths and festivals and helps not only the children to learn about each other but also the parents and the practitioners.

One family celebrated the Persian New Year, and this is something that the staff researched to gain an understanding. Children love it when staff refer to festivals that they celebrate with their families and communities and enjoy celebrating in the setting with their friends.

Figure 5.5 The many languages spoken at the setting are displayed in a positive way to celebrate difference.

Figure 5.6 A child enjoys decorating the Christmas tree as the setting prepares for the celebration.

Figure 5.7 Children help each other as they prepare for Christmas.

Figure 5.8 Religious and cultural festivals offer plenty of age-appropriate ways to introduce celebration.

Debbie and the staff at Parkside believe 'British values' is a positive phrase

Case study 2 – Lilleshall Primary School, Shropshire

The school is a small primary school in a predominately white, rural area. It is a faith based school. How does the school interpret British values and at the same time be an all-inclusive school to other religions and cultures? The head teacher, Christobel Cousins, and religious consultant Maria Hogan explain how the school interprets British values:

> We are an all-inclusive school as we do not see any religion or culture as the right one. We celebrate the difference that cultural diversity brings and ask that our pupils try to understand something before forming an opinion. It is our lack of understanding that breeds mistrust. To do this we use the cultural diversity within our school or access it in the wider community. We strive to ensure a balanced view and to discuss opinions held. British values underpin our society but without an understanding of life with/without them our pupils cannot value them. We need to look at what democracy offers us, what people have suffered/endured for us to have the right to vote. Then we begin to value our individual vote and see the power and importance of it. The rule of law, how this relates to school rules and enables us to work alongside each other in a community with structure and respect, but also how this links to the wider community and how laws are developed. Then pupils can understand the importance and role of the rule of law and therefore will be more likely to respect it. Individual liberty enables pupils to consider why your individual rights were established and how they will support and protect them as they go through life. British values are about understanding what we have and why. Once pupils have this knowledge they begin to value the key areas and see how they work in our society and this does not exclude any religion or culture.
>
> (Christobel Cousins, Head Teacher, Lilleshall
> Primary School, Shropshire)

Summary

Children need good attachments and a moral code if they are to grow into adults that are respectful and responsible. They need adults to role model this sense of right and wrong and support them in being responsible in their lives. This involves parents and practitioners working in partnership. Children can achieve a positive identity when they are given time to explore and make sense of the world and when they have positive key adults surrounding them.

British values are a set of core values that we, as a nation, need to follow and need to support our children in following to become a society that is tolerant, respectful of others, abides by rules and laws and one that promotes and celebrates uniqueness and diversity. There needs to a clear ethos that states what the setting believes in and places as its focus and British values are at the heart of this ethos.

The Early Years Foundation Stage curriculum puts into practice ways we can promote and celebrate together. Its four main themes of the unique child, positive relationships, the enabling environment and learning and development intertwine how we can implement the British values in all Early Years settings.

But British values in practice go deeper than the curriculum. It is inherent in the ethos and mission statement of the setting. It is in the policies on safe recruitment and confidentiality. It is demonstrated in a clear and reassuring key person system and it is in the way staff conduct themselves professionally.

British values in practice
Providing enabling environments and supporting learning and development

Children learn and develop well in enabling environments in which their experiences respond to their individual needs.

(DfE 2014b: 6)

The EYFS theme 3: the enabling environment

By creating environments that are respectful and tolerant of all cultures, faiths and beliefs, by finding out what we have in common and celebrating together, mutual respect and tolerance flourish. Before we embark on respecting 'other' faiths and beliefs as defined by British values, there is a necessity to be clear as to what is the country's dominant faith and belief. This is important as it is information that we can impart to parents especially as to why the focus of celebration may be certain traditions and customs as opposed to others.

Are we predominately a Christian country and, if so, should Christian values be the basis of British values?

Statistics would argue that Britain is no longer a Christian country, as the majority in Britain do not consider themselves Christian. There has been an increase in the number of people in Britain declaring they have no religion.

> The striking thing is the clear sense of the growth of 'no religion' as a proportion of the population.

(Stephen Bullivant, in Sherwood 2016)

Stephen Bullivant, senior lecturer in theology and ethics at St Mary's Catholic University in Twickenham, analysed data collected through British Social Attitudes surveys over three decades.

> The proportion of the population who identify in NatCen's British Social Attitudes survey as having no religion, referred to as 'nones', reached 48.5% in 2014, outnumbering the 43.8% who define themselves as Christian Anglicans, Catholics and other denominations.
>
> (Sherwood 2016)

However, this article was amended on 9 June 2016 to correct the subheading, which said that the proportion of the population who identify as having no religion rose from 25 per cent in 2011 to 48.5 per cent in 2014. That compared figures from two different sources: the 2011 census and NatCen's 2014 British Social Attitudes survey, which asked questions about religion in different ways (Office for National Statistics 2011; NatCen 2014). The 2011 BSA survey found 46 per cent identified as having no religion.

The starting point for faith

When considering identity, shared identity and respecting other faiths and beliefs, there is a question lurking overhead as to what belief is at the core. Traditions and festivals that are celebrated on a large scale in Britain continue to centre around the Christian faith. It is from this pretext that in this chapter the common traditions are defined. However, it is crucial to embrace other faiths and beliefs to truly follow the British values in practice. Other faiths and beliefs should be relevant to the community and setting but extend to celebrations found in the wider world. This is education at its best.

Celebrating British traditions, customs and festivals

Living in Britain means that there are customs and traditions based around religion or events that are a cause for celebrations. It is imperative that these traditions are not hijacked and celebrated in a negative, non-inclusive way. However, there is a need to have a starting point where Britain is saying this is what we celebrate as a country. For example, France celebrates Bastille Day and Ireland celebrates St Patrick's Day. There is also a need to celebrate new events and occasions as they occur. For example, the Olympics held in Britain in 2012 brought people together as a nation in the most positive way. The Queen's Jubilee was another example of events that occur in Britain. There are festivals that religions celebrate but what is wonderful to hear and see is that other faiths may join in. Some Hindu, Sikhs and Muslims may celebrate Christmas, not on the scale as a Christian, but they may take parts of it they know their children and families may enjoy. The opposite is also embraced. Many celebrate the festival of Holi, Chinese New Year or Eid and enjoy the experience and enjoy finding out about the different festivals.

Personal reflection

One of the loveliest, most colourful celebrations I took part in was the festival of Holi, and the children loved the colours of the paint as they swirled through the air. Celebrating religious festivals is just that: a celebration. It is a personal celebration to those who follow that faith but can be celebrated on a small scale throughout the community. There is no ulterior motive. Britain is very fortunate to have many opportunities to celebrate aspects of the different faiths in this country. Faith will be personal to that community or unique in the way it is celebrated in different families and aspects of it will be celebrated more fervently and this is where respect and tolerance need to shine.

Experiences individual to each family

Even within a faith, families may celebrate a holiday differently and so the role of the practitioner is to discover how families celebrate, what they can share and how they can include faith in learning. Early Years settings can ask parents to explain how they celebrate festivals; they may invite parents in to share the food they may eat on special occasions or the stories they may tell or the clothes they may wear.

Case study

The head teacher of Lilleshall Primary School in Shropshire, Christobel Cousins, feels that, although the school is a faith-based Christian school, it is imperative to celebrate and understand other religions. Many children are Christian but the school is open to all faiths.

'Enabling pupils with different religious beliefs to share how they celebrate their beliefs provides other pupils with a clear understanding of how that faith works in practice.' She also believes it has given her staff an insight into different faiths and beliefs.

Faith and prayer

Respect towards where and how people pray needs to be observed. For instance, prayer in the Muslim faith asks a believer to pray at a specific time during the day. This may have an impact on practitioners who are following this faith and may need time to pray during the day. Providing prayer rooms in the workplace gives people the opportunity to continue their religious observance that is important to them. These religious observances are examples of respect and tolerance that Britain has and should continue to have for all faiths. Settings may have specific parts of a faith that are intrinsically relevant to the setting. Many Catholic schools celebrate the feast day that their school is named after, such as St Joseph the Worker, St Teresa or St Scholastica. Jewish schools close early on a Friday to prepare for the Sabbath.

The dress code for different faiths may also be different for the people that practice that faith and again as where mutual tolerance and respect need to be apparent.

Some Christians wear a crucifix as an outward sign showing they follow a Christian belief; however, some people wear a crucifix because it is a piece of jewellery they like to wear. Some Muslims wear the hijab (a veil or scarf) because they see it as part of their faith; some may wear a colourful hijab or black hijab or some women may wear the full burkha (a long, loose garment covering the whole body from head to feet, worn in public by women in many Muslim countries). Again, this is preference or should be a preference and not demanded, showing how they wish to identify themselves.

In an Early Years setting, this may need to be addressed to parents or children as they may wish to understand. Often, assumptions are made and comments can be quite derogatory or discriminatory against these faith symbols. Stereotyping comes about through fear and assumptions, which leads to isolation and is contrary to British values in practice.

The starting point for celebrating

When celebrating festivals and occasions, practitioners need to start with what is the focus of celebrations where they are from, their locality. For example, settings by the beach may celebrate and give thanks to lifeguards and have customs known to the local area. Different parts of the country may celebrate certain feast days on a much larger scale than other parts of the country, for example, Burns Night in Scotland or St David's Day in Wales.

Mutual respect and tolerance for faiths and beliefs is celebrating together festivals that are inherently traditional in Britain and extending out to the community and celebrating the festivals and traditions that are part of the community that setting lives within.

When celebrating these occasions, it is essential to be aware that the history or original background behind the celebration may be deemed as insensitive to other cultures.

On 5 November, Guy Fawkes Night celebrates the burning of a rebellious Catholic. However, history is in the past. The present is what matters. When it is celebrated today, it is mainly about buying fireworks and enjoying the bright colours of the fireworks. It is important to remember that many nursery rhymes and traditional tales have meanings that may not be a cause for celebration as we perceive celebration now. These tales may have been part of traditions that now carry a different meaning. Even well-known and well-loved nursery rhymes or fairy stories have a dark meaning but are enjoyed by many now. The children's song 'Ring a ring o' roses' is about the small pox and death but it does not stop us singing it and enjoying the song with children. In fact, it is a playground favourite.

Changing the names of festivals because it may cause offence or be insensitive to other faiths is not the answer and often just fuels anger. Christmas is Christmas; it is not a winter festival. It may be a winter festival to others who are not Christian but it is Christmas to Christians and should not be changed. In fact, it causes more offence when the name is changed. The same respect needs to be given to practices that are important to other faiths. Celebrating traditions, customs and values returns to the clarity of identity. There are national festivities that have become part of the British culture. These may be celebrated in different ways through the personal identity of the communities. There are also many festivals and customs celebrated from the diverse communities that form Britain today. Celebration needs to include the personal, national and common identities that make up Britain.

Below is a list of the main celebrations in Britain today. The way that Early Years settings will celebrate these different traditions may be on a large or small scale depending on resources and location. The way that families within the Early Years setting celebrate thee festivals is also dependent on their faith, experiences, resources and preference.

Celebrations that are inherent in the British traditions

Christmas, Valentine's day, Shrove Tuesday (Pancake Day), Easter, Harvest, Halloween, Remembrance Sunday (Poppy Day)

Celebrations that may be relevant to large communities around Britain

St David's Day (Wales) St Patrick's Day (Northern Ireland) St Andrew's Day (Scotland), St George's Day (England), Burns Night.

Celebrations that may occur

The Queen's Jubilee, the Olympics hosted by the country.

Celebrations focused around sport

Football final, Cricket final, athletics, cycling.

Celebrations focused around charities

Coffee mornings for cancer charities, Red Nose Day or Children in Need.

And then there are the many customs from those whose identity and cultures have added a vibrancy and community feel to Britain.
For example, Notting Hill Carnival, Chinese New Year.

And festivals from other religions such as:
Hanukah, Diwali, Eid, Holi

This is not a list that is exhaustive or demands an order of importance. It shows the amount of celebrating that is welcomed in Britain today and enjoyed by so many and all these festivals and traditions have an **open invitation** to everyone within Britain.

Role of the Early Years practitioner in celebrating

The role of the Early Years setting is to start with what practitioners feel comfortable with, extending to what children and families have knowledge and experience of and further adding to celebrations that increases knowledge of the wider world.

Celebrating Christmas

Christmas is celebrated many ways throughout the world, and in Britain it is celebrated in various ways in different churches. Good practice in Early Years settings would be to find out how Christmas is celebrated amongst the families. It may be that the way that Christmas is celebrated in a different part of the world appeals to your setting.

Children love to decorate the Christmas tree. The origins of the Christmas tree tradition as we now know it started in Germany in the sixteenth century when devout Christians brought decorated trees into their homes.

British traditions may have their origins from different countries and people have adopted them into their traditions.

Remembrance Sunday in November is celebrated every year, and in every town, village and city in Britain is a memorial where poppies are laid to remember those who gave their lives through war so that we may have peace.

Figure 6.1 Mutual respect and tolerance for faiths and beliefs is celebrating together festivals that are inherently traditional in Britain and extending out to the community and celebrating the festivals and traditions that are part of the community that setting lives within.

Again, in Early Years settings, the message needs to be relevant to children. There may be great debates about the rights and wrongs of war, but the poppy has come to symbolise sacrifice and peace. It is one day in the year that enables a whole country to think about the importance of peace in our world today.

Celebration is one way to provide an enabling environment in the Early Years. Understanding the different customs and traditions of families within the setting provides an exciting and inclusive environment. But there are many ways that a setting can enhance and embrace cultures and traditions through daily practice.

Practitioners need to take time to get to know children and form partnerships with parents to enable a sense of community and belonging to foster and grow. There is a need to create an environment where children learn from the beginning what is meant by valuing and respecting each other. There is a need to celebrate diversity and experiences as learning about different cultures, customs and festivals that enhances our knowledge. The respect for diversity is right at the heart of what is most valued about living in Britain.

The goal of education in all diverse communities must therefore be to instil a sense of belonging to the wider community, and to the country in which they live.

The emotional environment

The emotional environment ensures that practitioners welcome every child in to the setting by supporting children with their personal social and emotional development, and practitioners have a duty to support them in growing and understanding the need to be aware of respect and tolerance of each other, understanding rules and managing behaviour and developing positive relationships with each other. There is a need for an enabling environment that is 'welcoming, inclusive and respectful' (Brodie 2014: 73). The emotional environment is linked directly to the unique child, which was addressed in the previous chapter.

The physical environment

Early Years settings need to vividly display an environment that celebrates diversity and demonstrates inclusiveness and that respects other faiths and beliefs. When referring to an enabling environment where children can learn and develop, it is common sense to begin at the beginning and consider the entrance of the setting. Learning takes many shapes and forms. And learning involves not only children but adults also, deepening their knowledge and understanding of what they know is important for children to learn. It is also important to look at the routines of the setting and how British values can be promoted and become part of everyday practice.

- How do areas such as toilets or kitchen areas also promote British values?
- Where are the rules of the setting displayed?
- Who is involved in making the rules?
- Last, British values can be apparent in many activities and experiences the children encounter.

What activities promote British values?

It is important to remember that the best place to start is with the children's needs and interests, with their customs, beliefs and traditions. This reiterates the ethos of a setting that is personal to that setting. But it is not good practice to remain there. An enabling environment needs to be just that, enabling children from a very young age to expand their learning and development, to learn about the wider world.

An inviting, welcome entrance

The entrance to every Early Years setting should proclaim a message of mutual respect and tolerance. The entrance creates an opportunity to display objects from the children's home, sharing customs and beliefs. It could be a talking point amongst parents. It may be objects from places that children have visited and again may be the start of conversations. The entrance that says welcome and shows mutual tolerance and respect should display a message that makes that setting unique and at the same time celebrate diversity.

The umbrella of diversity

The umbrella of diversity encapsulates who belongs to the setting. It celebrates the skills and qualities that individuals bring to the setting. It is personal to that setting. Just like an umbrella everyone can stand under it, sheltering each other even though they are all unique; all different.

Figure 6.2 The umbrella of diversity encapsulates who belongs to the setting. Just like an umbrella, everyone can stand under it, sheltering each other even though they are all unique, all different.

It is a display that could inform parents of the many diverse cultures within a setting. It could start with the workforce. From the many settings that I have had the privilege of working in, I have been so impressed at the commitment of the staff and the work ethic of the staff. When staff share their background or story, it makes it even more poignant how much work they have undertaken so that they can offer children in their care the best start.

The Early Years workforce is so varied but has the same aims and intentions when it comes to caring and educating children. The workforce can bring so many different qualities and skills to a setting that has a positive impact. Sometimes, knowing a little about the people that work in the setting may enable the manager to plan activities around the strengths and skills that practitioners bring to the setting. It is important to get to know staff and celebrate their uniqueness.

Hanging from the spikes of the umbrella could be information about the staff of the setting

For example, Simona works as a teaching assistant in the reception class. She supports children in their speech and confidence. She speaks English, Polish and Lithuanian. She was born in Lithuania and came to Britain with her husband as he worked here. She has two children who attend the school and has achieved her level 3 qualification. She enjoys cooking and takes responsibility for cooking activities in the 3–5-year-old room.

This sends a message to parents that the setting values their staff. It also sends a message to staff that they feel valued and their contributions are well thought of.

Staff need to feel valued in a setting and their culture or ethnicity seen as a positive impact on the children.

The umbrella of diversity is giving a clear message:

- We value our staff.
- We respect our staff and their differences.
- We work together for the benefit of the children in our care.
- We have many varied lives and skills and qualities that all add to the setting in a positive way.
- As parents, carers or visitors enter the setting, it should be obvious how children are cared for and by whom.

The umbrella of diversity could also be used to celebrate the children at the setting. It may show the different backgrounds of the children; it may be used to show the many countries the children have visited. It may advertise the different languages spoken or the varied festivals celebrated.

The welcome tree of tolerance

Many settings may be a faith based setting or may have only a few different cultures or races. However, it is still vital to proclaim the message of mutual respect and tolerance.

Displaying the rules and the message of British values

In the foyer or entrance of a setting, practitioners proclaim a message. Usually displayed are the rules and policies of the setting, the registration details. This reassures parents that policies are in place to keep their children safe.

Figure 6.3 The tree of tolerance.

However, the message may sometimes be lost because it is paper based and there is lots of it. Busy parents who drop children off in the morning have many pressures and so vivid displays can entice them to look. Displaying policies in a vivid way may enable parents to take notice. Involving parents in decision making such as giving them opportunities for evaluating the setting enables parents feel that they belong to the setting.

Children and parents need to be involved in the decision-making processes, for example, participating in the rules of the setting and displaying these rules on the backdrop of the welcome tree. A tree of welcome could display the many words of learning that we want to instil in our young children. Perhaps during the settling in time, or meetings, parents can add to this tree and even children can add to the tree what they value.

Practitioners can ensure that children understand their own and others' behaviour and its consequences, and learn to distinguish right from wrong. They should encourage a range of experiences that allow children to explore the language of feelings and responsibility, reflect on their differences and understand we are free to have different Learning and development understanding the world

Posters that depict the welcome of all families and the different family structures send out a clear message of tolerance.

It is vital that the setting has strategies in place to break down these barriers and so policies need to be clear about when practitioners are available to talk to parents.

The open-door policy

The open-door policy needs to be just that and practitioners need to reflect on the impact and success of the open-door policy by asking themselves are they welcome and approachable to all parents and carers.

- Does the setting offer open days and open evenings?
- Is there an opportunity to celebrating good practice and share observations?
- Are the observations from the setting linked to what the child can do at home?
- How do parents who work and may not be able to attend day meetings or sessions communicate with key persons about their child's progress?
- How do parents who have English as an additional language (EAL) and find it difficult to understand have access to information?
- How does the setting reassure parents who may have a very negative of school themselves and find it hard to talk to adults in the setting as they feel negative?

Opportunities for family learning and family information

Does the setting enable parents to access classes to improve parenting skills and gain qualifications?

Figure 6.4 British values of democracy, individual liberty, rule of law and mutual respect and tolerance should be displayed in a child- and parent-friendly way.

Are there systems in place to support parents when they arrive from different countries for whatever reason?

Routines that provide opportunities to promote British values

A display in the toileting area on the words children use may help all staff to be aware of the child's needs if English is an additional language or if the child is attempting words and attempting to vocalise words. For example, children that are being potty trained may use a word from their home language that needs to be recognised by all staff.

There could be a display in the kitchen to show how names of fruit or food is used from home language or words that children are using to express their needs.

All this helps and supports independence but it also shows a setting that is sensitive to the unique needs of their children.

The environment that promotes tolerance and respect is only successful if its message is transferred to the home setting. The message of tolerance and respect needs to filter through to families and be reinforced at home for British values to be effective. And the environment needs to set up a place of learning that also promotes the British values.

The EYFS theme 4: learning and development

> Children develop and learn in different ways. The framework covers the education and care of all children including children with special educational needs and disabilities.
>
> (DfE 2014b)

Links with British values

Rule of law

By facilitating children in their learning and development from a very early age, by teaching them boundaries and right from wrong, by supporting them in learning how to negotiate and share and take turns and in how to resolve conflict, they are gaining the understanding of the rule of law. Learning involves an understanding that there is a need for a set of rules to abide by, again adhering to the UNCRC article 14 'children have the right to think what they want' knowing that with this comes responsibility 'to ensure that while enjoying these rights, they do not stop others enjoying theirs' (Sargent 2016: 9).

Mutual tolerance of respect of other faiths and beliefs

A limited approach is sometimes considered acceptable when encouraging mutual respect and tolerance. However, it is not acceptable to have this limited approach that could easily be viewed as tokenistic. Children from a very early age need to understand that there is a wider world that they are part of and need to include in their learning and development.

The activities below link to the EYFS and promote British values in a positive way.

Table 6.1 Focus area: understanding the world

Birth–20 months	(Links to PSED) enjoys company of others recognises and responds to main carers	The welcoming environment
	Likes cuddles, uses eye contact to make contact with people	
16–26 months	Is curious about people and shows an interest in stories about themselves, their families and other people	Include books, posters and resources that reflect positive images of all children
22–36 months	Imitates life actions from own family and cultural background	Use props, puppets and dolls to tell stories about diverse experiences ensuring that negative stereotyping is avoided
	Learns they have similarities and differences that connect them	
30–60 months	Remembers significant events	Visits to different parts of the community
	Shows an interest in different occupations	Provide role play areas with a variety of different resources
		Displays that reflect the community
		Invite children and families with experiences of living in other countries to bring in photos or objects

Early learning goal

Children talk about past and present events in their own lives and the lives of family members. They know that other children don't always enjoy the same things and are sensitive to this. They know about similarities and differences between themselves and others and among families' communities and traditions

Learning and development

Opening the world with different experiences is the essence of supporting children to learn about the wider world they live in. There is a need to bring that wider world to them.
   Practitioners need to ask:

Has the child ever visited a farm, the beach or a museum to increase vocabulary?

Have they opportunities to look at things unfamiliar to them and comment on what they do or what they can see or feel or smell?

Has the child had experiences of what it means to celebrate with family, friends and others? Has the child had the opportunity to taste different foods, to listen to different music and to hear different stories?

Other ways to respect and tolerate different faiths and beliefs are to celebrate and share art work, music and stories and food that come from the traditions of those faiths and cultures.

Activities that respect and tolerate different faiths and beliefs:

- **Appreciating different art and artists, music and musicians**
- **Using puppets and props to retell stories**
- **Learning through the community**
- **Enjoying the food and drink the celebrations bring**

Music, story activities and food are great focuses to start introducing and respecting different cultures and customs.

Table 6.2 Expressive art and design (EAD), communication and language (CL) and physical development (PD) are great focus areas to start introducing and respecting different cultures and customs

Age	EAD Exploring using media and materials	EAD Being imaginative	CL Listening and attention	PD Health and self-care
Birth–11 months	Plays and explores characteristics of effective learning	Listens to familiar sounds, words or finger plays	Is physically active, making eye contact, using touch or voice to enable baby to listen and attend	Respond to cultural needs and expectations of skin and hair care, ensuring parents' wishes are respected Find out food preferences and dietary requirements
8–26 months	Moves whole body to sound they enjoy such as music or a regular beat	Concentrates intently on an object or activity of own choosing for short periods	Has a strong exploratory impulse	Help children enjoy their food, try different flavours and textures by combining favourites with new tastes and textures
22–36 months	Joins in singing favourite songs Creates sounds by banging	Pretends one object represents another Begins to make believe by pretending	Listens intently to the noises adults make when they read a story Recognises and responds to many familiar sounds	Discuss cultural expectations for personal care (in some cultures some young boys may be used to sitting rather than standing) Respond to how child communicates need for food drinks and toileting

Age	EAD Exploring using media and materials	EAD Being imaginative	CL Listening and attention	PD Health and self-care
30–50 months	Taps out rhythms Sings a few familiar songs Enjoys joining in with dancing and ring games Explores different sounds of music	Notices what adults do, imitating what is observed and then doing it spontaneously when the adult is not there Engages in imaginative role play based on first hand experiences Builds stories around toys Uses available resources to create props for toys Plays alongside or as part of a group with other children	Listens to others with increasing attention and recall Can follow directions Maintains concentration	Be sensitive to varying family expectation and life patterns when encouraging thinking about health Children know the importance of good health and physical exercise

Figure 6.5 British values in practice runs throughout the Early Year's curriculum.

The early learning goals are the goals that children are progressing towards and practitioners want to support them to achieve. The early learning goals can link directly to British values and activities that promote British values are described below to help children achieve these early learning goals in the setting

Focus activities to promote British values in personal social and emotional development (PSED)

Turn taking games

Construction activities, building together

Deciding on the rules of the group

Persona dolls and puppets

Expressions to identify how they are feeling today

Circle time

Mindfulness and yoga

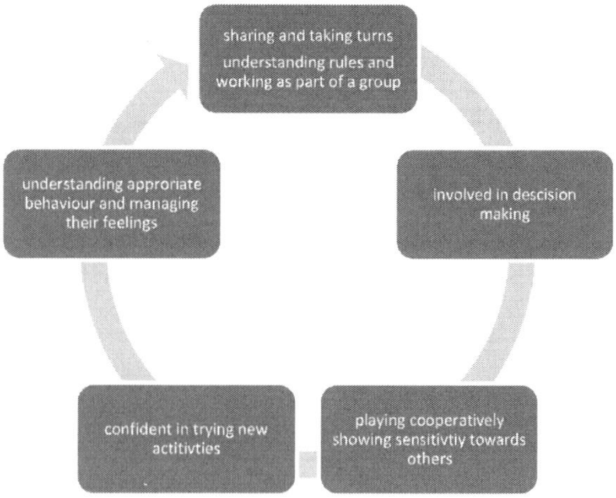

sharing and taking turns
understanding rules and working as part of a group

understanding approriate behaviour and managing their feelings

involved in descision making

confident in trying new actitivties

playing cooperatively showing sensitivtiy towards others

Focus activities to promote British values in Communication and Language (CL)

Show and tell

Making up their own stories

Story time

Music time

Giving children areas for responsibility

Tidy up time

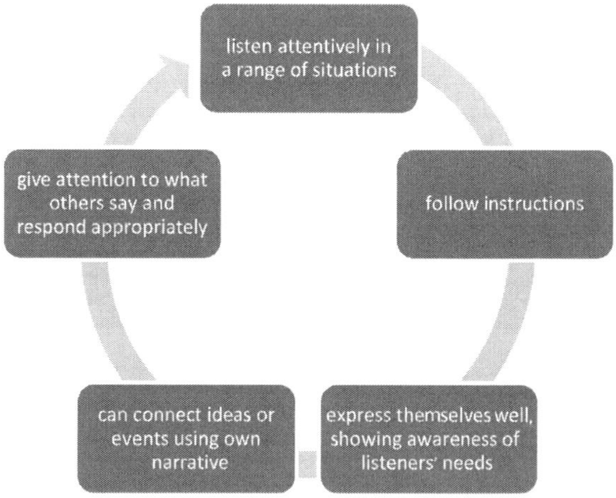

listen attentively in a range of situations

give attention to what others say and respond appropriately

follow instructions

can connect ideas or events using own narrative

express themselves well, showing awareness of listeners' needs

Activities that promote British values in Physical Development (PD)

Snack time

Lunch time

Personal routines

Outdoor play

Outdoors in the local area

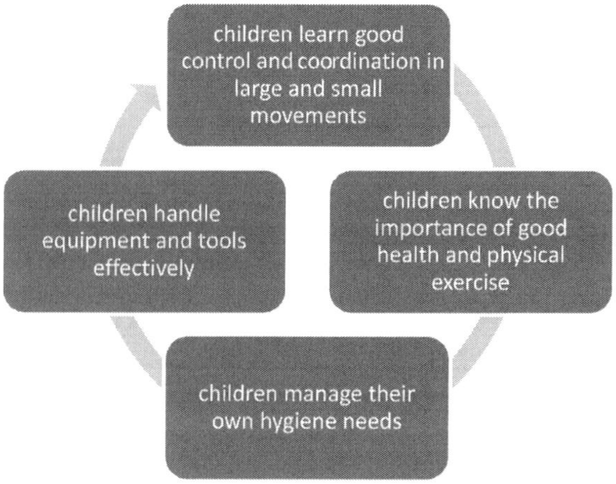

children learn good control and coordination in large and small movements

children handle equipment and tools effectively

children know the importance of good health and physical exercise

children manage their own hygiene needs

Figure 6.6 Examples of focused activities that promote British values.

Table 6.3 The specific areas

Literacy	Maths	Understanding the world	Expressive arts and design
Children learn and understand simple sentences. They use phonics to decode regular words and can read common irregular words.	Children count reliably from one to 20, place the numbers in order and can add and subtract two single digit numbers. They solve problems including doubling, halving and sharing.	Children talk about past events in their own lives. They know that other children don't always enjoy the same things and are sensitive to this. They know about similarities and differences between themselves and others, and among families, communities and traditions.	Children sing songs, make music and dance. They safely use a variety of material and tools experimenting with colour, design, textures.
Children use phonic knowledge to write words and simple sentences that can be read by themselves and others.	Children use everyday language to talk about size, weight capacity, distance, time and money. They create patterns and explore shapes using mathematical language to describe them.	Children talk about features of their immediate environment. They make observations of animals and plants and explain why some things occur and talk about changes. They recognise a range of technology is used in places and select technology for purposes.	Children use what they have learnt about media and materials in original ways, thinking about uses and purposes. They represent their own ideas, thought and feelings, through design and technology, art, music, dance role play and stories.

Summary

One of the key messages of British values is the importance of mutual respect and tolerance of different faiths and beliefs. To understand clearly the term different faiths, there is a need to realise what is the central focus. Recent statistics show the focus may not be as clear cut as it once was. Britain is no longer viewed as a Christian country as many people define themselves as having no religion. However, Britain has kept the traditions and customs that have been based around the Christian faith or events in history. This must be the starting point. Celebrations also encompass other faiths and new events, such as the Olympics or the Queen's Jubilee, that Britain has enjoyed celebrating. It also includes sporting events or events local to communities.

Early Years settings need to start with the community they exist in. They need to celebrate festivals, traditions and customs local to their setting as well as discovering about the different customs throughout Britain. Britain is fortunate to have such diverse and colourful experiences. Customs and traditions bring with it stories, art, food and music that again are great learning experiences for children from a young age.

> A fully inclusive setting will acknowledge, respect, include and provide for children and families of all faiths, beliefs and cultures. It will also provide respect for people from different genders, ages, sexualities and with disabilities. This will be reflected in an inclusive ethos and cohesive learning community.
>
> (Sargent 2016: 48)

7 | The meaningful neighbour

British values' main aim is to find a bond that encapsulates a sense of togetherness. Practitioners and families cannot be cocooned into a false sense of belonging by solely limiting children's experiences to the setting. There is a need to return to grass roots communities and consider examples of how we can support British values in practice in the wider community. When considering the meaningful neighbour, two approaches come to mind and both have roots in different countries.

Te Whāriki

The Te Whāriki approach emphasises the learning partnership between teachers, parents, and families. The approach perceives the role of the professional is to weave a holistic curriculum in response to children's learning and development in the early childhood setting and the wider context of the child's world.

> Each community to which a child belongs, whether it is a family home or an early childhood setting outside the home, provides opportunities for new learning to be fostered: for children to reflect on alternative ways of doing things; make connections across time and place; establish different kinds of relationship; and encounter different points of view. These experiences enrich children's lives and provide them with the knowledge, skills, and dispositions they need to tackle new challenges.
>
> (Ministry of Education 2016)

The Reggio Emilia approach

The essence of this approach is to foster children to learn and develop and become responsible and caring citizens. For this to be successful, children must see this in practice. The approach believes the community impacts on a child's learning. It was founded by Lori Malaguzzi after the Second World War and was a response to the devastation that was seen in the province of Reggio Emilia, which is one of the nine provinces in Italy known as Emilia Romagna. There was a need for hope for the children, and the community set about making schools and learning available to the children who were surrounded by bombed out buildings.

From the rubble grew a very new way of learning, involving the community in a child's learning.

In the same way, British values are a response to the negative and often brutal assumptions made that have led to division in society. The emotional destruction that now suffocates our young children needs to be addressed on a much larger scale for it to be effective and successful in the long term. Children cannot be cocooned; they live in the real world and so will face many things in the real world. It is the role of practitioners and parents to foster that sense of belonging not just at home or in the setting but within the community. The skills acquired in the Early Years settings need to be the firm foundation for when they start school to help them understand what it means to work together, follow the rules of a society whilst respecting freedom of expression and tolerating others, namely the British values.

Settings need to involve the communities that the children live in to extend the children's understanding of what it means to care for others and feel a real sense of belonging. Learning needs to take place that involves the community. For an Early Years setting to be successful in promoting British values in a positive way, it must extend out to the community. Practitioners, parents and children must be visible in the community.

The young child needs to be visible in his or her community. The Early Years setting needs to be a central focus in the community.

Here are some examples of how this can be achieved.

Involving older people

Many children may have grandparents that they enjoy spending their time with. However, some children may not, and some older members of the community may only ever experience children when they see them being loud and rude on bus journeys or in shops. This leads to perceptions being distorted or generalised. Opportunities for young and old people to meet in a positive way could lead to a more positive understanding of each other. In the article 'Old People's Homes: Everything that is Right in the World' Goorwich writes that one residence's website 'explains that the children and residents come together in a variety of planned activities such as music, dancing, art, lunch, storytelling' and that these activities have positive effects for both parties. It is set in Seattle, USA, but can be easily adapted to settings here (Goorwich 2015).

Visiting an allotment in the community

Another example of learning in the community for our youngest members of society is to own or visit an allotment in the community.

Gardening and growing fruit or vegetables is linked to well-being. Allotments also 'bring together people from different cultural and ethnic backgrounds whose knowledge of gardening can be shared' (Wiltshire and Burn 2009).

For personal, social and emotional development and indeed physical development, learning can be immense. At the same time, children are learning to care for the environment. Many Early Years settings now have their own growing area and share the food that they grow, which again is an opportunity to bring people together.

Taking pride in the local community

Children learn from a very early age what is acceptable and unacceptable in society. Being responsible for tidying up activities is a responsibility engrained in children from a young age. But, often, transferring this skill to tidying up in the community is lost. There are many ways children can be visible in the community. Many Early Years settings are central to the community and so need to be part of that community. Posters exhibited in train stations, bus stops or shops sending out messages of how the setting supports responsibility in young children give a subtle message to the community as to how they can continue this practice.

All settings need to start with what is important and relevant to their community but realise that children live and will grow up to be a part of the wider community and the world. Early Years education is laying foundations where children accept, understand and tolerate those that are different, seeing uniqueness as a vibrant and colourful addition to community.

Summary

A child cannot have wonderful positive relationships and experiences in the setting and then go home and live within a community that instils negativity and aggression towards those people that may be different. It is not only the responsibility of practitioners and parents to support a child in their development but also the responsibility of a community. From an early age, children need to see within the community good role models as their behaviour and outlook will have an influence and impact on a child's learning. The way a person behaves on a bus or in a shop will have an impact on a child's learning and perception of the world. The whole of the child's environment needs to be considered if learning and promoting British values is to be truly successful. The unique child needs to be visible to the community that they live in and the community needs to be visible to the unique child if British values in practice are to be effective and successful.

Reflecting on our own values and attitudes

Inclusion refers to 'equality of opportunity for all pupils regardless of their ethnicity, culture, language, ability, attainment, age or gender' (Moyles, 2007: 48). Moyles argues that inclusion should not be limited to policy but needs a pedagogical approach for practitioners to be successful in their teaching.

A pedagogical approach

A pedagogical approach involves how practitioners can support real learning in enabling environments where children can grow and develop. 'It is concerned not just with knowing about things, but also with changing ourselves and the world we live in' (Smith 2016).

For this reason, it is imperative that practitioners are professional and approachable to all children and families that belong to their setting. For this to happen, practitioners need to have a positive outlook and acceptance of those communities that feel isolated.

'Early childhood pedagogy is underpinned by passionate commitment' (Osgood 2006 cited in Moyles 2007: 49). It involves 'empathetic engagement, and personal involvement with children, their families and communities' (Moyles 2007: 49).

The whole profession needs to have a similar commitment to this professional and positive attitude to all children.

'Children need a lot of adult guidance to appreciate the views and feelings of others' (Pugh and Duffy 2014: 189) and 'if children see us showing kindness, patience, love, empathy, respect and care for others, they are more likely to want to emulate such behaviours' (Pugh and Duffy 2014: 189).

For this to be effective in practice, practitioners need to see all communities in a positive light and be professional in their approach towards them.

Sometimes this can prove difficult, especially if rumours or assumptions suffocate the truth; negative, stereotypical attitudes occur as a direct result of misinformation. There is an unrest in many communities today, as many believe that immigration has escalated and it is perceived as a key setback to the problems encountered in settings. There is also an assumption that children whose first language is not English are draining the resources of classrooms and nurseries up and down the country, and there are still some ethnic groups that are marginalised or feel isolated because of the way they choose to live.

If the role of the practitioner is to foster a sense of belonging, this must include groups that feel on the outside. Practitioners need to have a positive outlook and use strategies to foster belonging and not add to the barriers that see confrontations towards such groups. When studying for a qualification in Early Years, students are asked to reflect on their own attitudes and values as part of their coursework. Therefore, in this chapter, I have included some information on these supposed problems and the myths surrounding them.

The question of immigration

The fear of alienation and discrimination leads to exploitation and radicalisation if people feel that they do not belong. Failure to include certain groups in society is often a result of these groups being overlooked and their vulnerability overlooked. As practitioners, there is a need to discover what will help us improve outcomes for all children in our care.

> Our country is simmering with anger and frustration. There is no shortage of social grievances that, long unaddressed by politicians, are a source of considerable bitterness. But if the problem is a housing shortage or less jobs, immigrants are always blamed for the troubles.
>
> (Jones 2016)

Because of this misconception, we often fail the most needy and vulnerable groups in our society. Immigration is not the cause for all the problems in Britain today. And it is certainly not the obstacle limiting educational progression. The five outcomes are not hampered by immigration. They could be deemed hindered by lack of funding, poverty or failing children who have specific needs.

Every Child Matters

If every child matters, then, as practitioners, we need to believe it. As practitioners, we need to examine and reflect on our own attitudes and we know how to access correct and honest information. There are many myths and little known facts that influence perception of immigration. When promoting British values, it is vital that the ethos and principles that underpin British values are meant for everyone. Sometimes it seems as if history repeats itself and negativity rises often based on myths or assumptions or stereotyping. As adults, we are all entitled to our opinion but to voice that opinion and not have it backed up by facts will have a tremendous impact on practice.

Settings need to take a stance on attitudes

Saying 'we don't do that here' or 'we don't say that here' gives a message to children, staff and parents that the setting promotes equality and anti-discriminatory practice. The message heard is:

We respect everyone's right to be here in our setting. We follow and abide by the rules. We want to promote good manners, politeness, respect and tolerance and so we need to role model this to all our parents and children and indeed in the wider community.

> The Early Years staff need to offer all children guidance and support in developing positive attitudes towards all people.
>
> (Pugh and Duffy 2014: 188)

The adult has an enormous influence on children's learning and behaviour:

> In the Early Years children are vulnerable and every adult has the power to affect each child's future actions and behaviour, as well as their intentions, learning outcomes and beliefs.
>
> (Pugh and Duffy 2014: 182)

Myths start from not knowing and fear. It may be from something that has been read or something that has been heard and possibly misinterpreted. Table 8.1 shows some of the myths around immigration.

The Organisation for Economic Co-operation and Development published a report that showed that immigration makes a positive contribution to the public finances of many countries, including Britain. However, as a nation we still, at times, have a negative attitude towards immigrants that come to this country.

Table 8.1 Myths and facts regarding immigration

Fact	Myth
Migrants in the UK pay more tax than they consume in public services (That's not true of every migrant of course, but collectively they make a net contribution.) Without them, we would have to make further cuts to public services or pay higher taxes or both.	Foreigners don't pay taxes.
Immigration helps us deal with our debt GDP per head is essentially a measure of productivity. Nobody is claiming immigration significantly increases that. What the evidence shows is that it boosts GDP itself – the size of our economy. And because migrants tend to be younger and more economically active than the population (this is, of course, a generalisation – the reality is that some types of immigration are more economically beneficial than others, of which more shortly), it also helps us deal with our debt problem at least in the short to medium term.	They are putting our country into more debt.
76 per cent of Romanians and Bulgarians who arrived in the UK last year came for work That compares with 61 per cent of people from the original 15 EU members and 67 per cent of people from the eight eastern European countries that joined the bloc in 2004. Popular perceptions are different: In a report analysing language used by 19 British national newspapers in the two years preceding the lifting of a seven-year ban on employment, Oxford University's Migration Observatory said that words used to describe immigrants were largely derogatory, which only inflamed hatred and rejection of immigrants in to communities	All Romanians and Bulgarians are thieves and steal from shops. Romanians frequently evoked crime and anti-social behaviour, especially in the tabloid press.
British workers are British born (mostly) Foreign-born residents make up almost 16 per cent of the 31 million-strong labour force. Of the total number of overseas workers, 60 per cent were born outside the EU, 16 per cent are from western Europe, while 15 per cent are from eastern Europe. The two poorest EU countries, Romania and Bulgaria, accounted for 3.8 per cent of workers.	There are too many foreigners here. People are coming over here and taking all our jobs.
Most people vying to settle in Britain come from outside the trading bloc. The top two arriving nationalities are, in fact, *Chinese and Indian*.	Most plumbers in England are Polish.
Most immigrants come to work Foreign arrivals come mostly to work or study and about two-thirds of those moving for employment already have job offers when they arrive, even as politicians decry 'benefit tourism'. In researcher NatCen's British Social Attitudes Survey, taken in 2013 and published in June 2014, 24 per cent of respondents said they believed welfare was the most common motive for migration when that was listed as one of the choices.	Most immigrants just want our benefits.
While legal foreign residents are eligible for social welfare, **93 per cent of the 5.3 million people claiming aid, such as Jobseekers' Allowance and disability benefits, have British nationality**	
Immigration has become a scapegoat for all problems. Problems are due to other causes but immigration has become an easy scapegoat when for them it has minimal impact on the issues they face.	Immigration is the problem in this country.

Here are some common "myths" you may have heard about immigration. Do you know what's true and what isn't?

Myth: Immigrants move to new countries to get on welfare, unemployment, or other "free money" programs.

Fact: People usually move to new countries in search of honest work for decent pay. Most immigrants work and pay taxes, so they help their new nation's economy rather than hurt it.

Myth: Immigrants take jobs away from people who already live in a country.

Fact: In some cases, new arrivals in a country do compete for jobs with people already living there. But more often, new immigrants take low-paying jobs that others don't want, or create their own businesses and jobs.

Myth: Most immigrants sneak into a new country illegally.

Fact: In the United States, two out of three new immigrants have either permanent or temporary legal status, meaning they're absolutely allowed to be in the country. Of the one-third of immigrants who are undocumented, about half of them entered the U.S. through a legal way, and the other half crossed the border secretly.

Myth: When people move to new countries, they bring crime with them.

Fact: Statistics show that in the U.S., immigrants are less likely to commit crimes than native-born Americans.

Myth: Immigrants don't want to learn the language and culture of their new country.

Fact: It can be hard to learn a new language and adapt to a new culture, especially for older adults. But most immigrants understand that learning the native language and customs can help them fit in, and even get better jobs. Younger immigrants and the children of immigrants usually find it easier to adapt

Myth: Immigrants aren't interested in becoming citizens of their new nation.

Fact: Many immigrants apply for citizenship, but depending on the laws of their new country, this can be a long and complicated process. Often, a person must live in a nation for many years before becoming a citizen is even an option.

But research continues to show there is a substantial gap between what the public thinks to be true and what the reality of the situation is.

The charts below show some information on immigration and have been adapted from 'Nine of the Most Surprising Facts about Immigration' (Allegretti 2015).

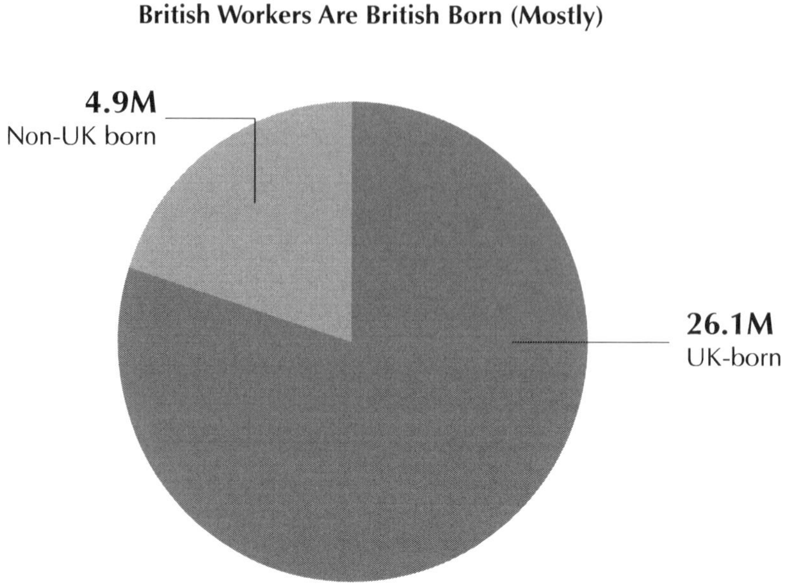

British Workers Are British Born (Mostly)

4.9M
Non-UK born

26.1M
UK-born

Figure 8.1 The majority of British workers are British born.
Source: UK Office for National Statistics Labor Force Survey January-March 2015

Why are people immigrating to the UK?

The most common reason for migrating to the UK is work. This has been the case historically, except for 2009 to 2012, when formal study was the most common main reason for migration.

In the year ending June 2015, a total of 294,000 immigrated for work-related reasons. This is a statistically significant increase from the previous year when 241,000 people immigrated for work-related reasons. Of those immigrating for work-related reasons in the year ending June 2015, 64 per cent (187,000) came with a definite job to go to and 36 per cent (107,000) came to look for work.

There were increases in immigration for work among EU citizens and non-EU citizens. Provisional estimates from the International Passenger Survey (IPS) from the Office for National Statistics (see https://www.ons.gov.uk/) show that 58 per cent (162,000) were EU citizens (excluding British citizens), which was not a statistically significant increase and 24 per cent (67,000) were non-EU citizens, also not a statistically significant increase from the previous year. Most other sources also show that immigration for work has increased over the last year for both EU and non-EU citizens.

The second most common reason for immigrating to the UK was formal study. In the year ending June 2015, a total of 192,000 people immigrated to the UK for formal study. Provisional estimates from the IPS show that the majority (131,000 or

71 per cent) were non-EU citizens while 47,000 (24 per cent) were EU citizens (excluding British citizens).

In the year ending June 2015, a total of 80,000 people arrived in the UK to accompany or join others, this remains relatively unchanged from 82,000 the previous year. Provisional estimates from the IPS show that the majority (45,000 or 58 per cent) were non-EU citizens while 23,000 (30 per cent) were EU citizens (excluding British citizens).

After a year of remaining in this country it is considered that Britain will now be classed as their home and the country they left they will be defined as an emigrant.

Foreign-born residents make up almost 16 per cent of the 31 million-strong labour force. Of the total number of overseas workers, 60 per cent were born outside the EU; 16 per cent are from western Europe, while 15 per cent are from eastern Europe. The two poorest EU countries, Romania and Bulgaria, accounted for 3.8 per cent of workers.

In fact, the British public overestimates the share of immigrants in the total population: respondents to a poll by Ipsos MORI earlier this year guessed it was 21 per cent. The actual figure is 13 per cent, according to the UK's Office of National Statistics.

Foreign arrivals come mostly to work or study and about two-thirds of those moving for employment already have job offers when they arrive, even as politicians decry 'benefit tourism'. In researcher NatCen's British Social Attitudes Survey, taken

Foreign Workers Come from Everywhere

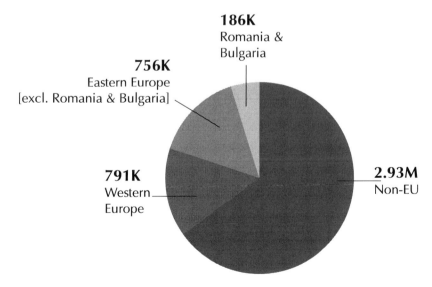

Figure 8.2 Foreign workers come to work in Britain from all around the globe.
Source: UK Office for National Statistics Labor Force Survey January–March 2015

Benefit Recipients

Foreigners from the EU account for a tiny fraction of those who get social aid

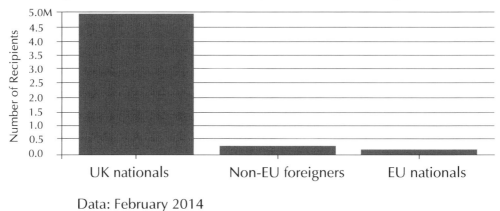

Data: February 2014

Figure 8.3 People from the EU account for a tiny fraction of those who get social aid.
Source: UK Department for Work and Pensions

in 2013 and published in June 2014, 24 per cent of respondents said they believed welfare was the most common motive for migration when that was listed as one of the choices.

While legal foreign residents are eligible for social welfare, 93 per cent of the 5.3 million people claiming aid, such as Jobseekers' Allowance and disability benefits, have British nationality.

Why is this information important?

It is important to keep up to date with facts as practitioners needs to stand alongside the most vulnerable parents and children who may be open to abuse, bullying or isolation just because of what has been read in a newspaper that day. Keeping up to date with facts is important if we are to work with children and families. First, it gives you an honest understanding of events. Second, this will reflect in your attitude. When you know sometimes the struggles that families have coped with, it enables you to empathise with their predicament.

Settings need an empathy towards immigrants arriving in the community, and to show support in helping them to find information that can enable them to live here without feeling fearful of their future.

New families from different countries that settle here contribute to Britain. They become part of the workforce, they add a vibrancy and diversity to celebrations and festivals and they bring their home language to further extend knowledge and learning.

EAL workforce members and children are a beneficial addition to our education system

One further myth that I would like to clarify is the assumption that English as an additional language (EAL) learners or practitioners with EAL cause a low level of English in our schools. Children with English as an additional language do not hold back other children in a setting. It often materialises that they can speak several languages and yet it is brought into conversation as a negative aspect. EAL adults are at different levels in their English acquisition. Some may be new to English and some may have good command of spoken English but may need support with written English or understanding terminology in the course. Others are extremely competent in their understanding and their formal written English. It has made me realise that you cannot bracket EAL learners under one umbrella, and from working with many parents who speak many languages I have realised that acquiring a good standard of English is achievable.

Parents that come to us want to work with children and want to learn strategies and the rules of the English language so that they can support their own children at home as well as children in the setting. They have an empathy for children whose first language may not be English and could be a real asset to a setting showing children and their parents that learning English is a skill that is never too late to learn.

We have a human resource that I believe we are just not using effectively and often, as teachers, may not know the best way. Whilst EAL students are striving to be proficient in English, they have a skill that we need to tap into.

The National Association of Language Development In the Curriculum (NALDIC) publishes statistics regarding the number of children with EAL. The percentage of the primary school population in the UK with English as an additional language (EAL) has risen year-on-year from 10 per cent in 2002 to just under 18 per cent in 2012 (NALDIC 2012).

In the Key Stage 2 (KS2) tests in 2011, on a national scale, 70 per cent of pupils whose first language is not English achieved the expected levels in both English and mathematics. For pupils whose first language is English, the percentage was 75 per cent (DfE 2011).

For inner London, the picture is somewhat different (NALDIC 2012): 54 per cent of the primary school population are pupils whose first language is not English. In the 2011 KS2 tests, 76 per cent of inner London pupils with EAL achieved the expected level or above, compared with 77 per cent of pupils whose first language is English. This pattern continues to the end of KS4 where 61.0 per cent of pupils whose first language is other than English achieved five or more GCSE grades A–C compared with 61.7 per cent of pupils whose first language is English (NALDIC 2012).

Having another language does not hinder progress.

'In 2013, 44 per cent of EAL and bilingual children achieved a good level of development in the EYFS compared with 54 per cent of children whose first language is English' (NALDIC 2012).

A positive attitude to EAL learners may ensure they have the motivation and confidence to succeed. The statutory framework states that for children, whose home language is not English, providers must take reasonable steps to provide opportunities for children to develop and use the home language in play and learning (DfE 2014b).

The following key points summarise why, where possible, it is important to seek bilingual support: Children who speak little or no English at home may be at a disadvantage when they enter an Early Years setting without some support in the language with which they are most familiar. For a child who has limited understanding of English, opportunities to use their home language can be like turning on a light in a dark room; the setting and all its possibilities are opened.

Practitioners need to find out essential information about a child's competency in the home language, which will inform your expectations of their learning needs.

For parents, it may be a real relief to be able to communicate with practitioners via first language support, to have an opportunity to inform practitioners about their child's care, learning needs and achievements, and to find out about the aims and values of the setting.

We know that EAL children can be successful. We know that EAL children need learning opportunities to speak in their own language as well as learning English as it gives them confidence and promotes a good self-esteem. The Department for Education for Children, Families and Schools (2007) found that children learning EAL are as able as any other children, and the learning experiences planned for them should be no less challenging. Additional visual support is vital for children learning English and using illustration and artefacts will also support and enhance the learning experiences of their monolingual peers. Many children go through a 'silent phase' when learning a new language; this may last for several months but is not usually a cause for concern and is not a passive stage.

The statutory framework for the Early Years Foundation Stage states: 'Providers must ensure that staff have sufficient understanding and use of English to ensure the well-being of children in their care' (DfE 2014b, point 3.26 Safeguarding and welfare requirement).

But we also need to have a clear and honest understanding of the facts and statistics surrounding the groups that make up our community and the groups within different communities that are considered vulnerable or that the system is failing. We need to acknowledge the many cultures and customs within our community, pay attention to those that may feel alienated or vulnerable and improve outcomes for those that we are failing. Fostering a sense of belonging and promoting identity and self-esteem are a major part of the aims that need to be at the forefront of planning in the Early Years.

Summary

Accessing honest facts is a responsibility of the practitioner in the Early Years setting that is imperative to good practice. Practitioners need to reflect on their own attitudes and opinions as it will have an impact on the quality of their practice.

Every child is unique and needs to be cared for and educated so that their development progresses and their learning is wide and varied.

Information regarding immigration and EAL learners should not be based on rumour or blamed for the standards in the education system.

Supportive, welcoming environments where there is partnership with all parents and children from the outset leads to a positive, inclusive society where we learn from each other.

9 | Concluding thoughts

The concept of British values has been introduced to the Early Years curriculum with mixed feelings. Some have viewed it as a negative concept that may further isolate communities that live and work in Britain. Many believe that it should be referred to as human values. I hope, in this book, that I have addressed these concerns and reflected how the concept of British values in practice is a positive step to defining Britain as an inclusive and welcoming society.

From an early age, young children need to make sense of the world and they make sense of the world by forming an identity. This identity is personal to them. It includes their culture, customs, beliefs and ethnicity that they grow and develop in. Identity also needs to extend to a shared identity where children and families realise that they belong to a society that welcomes uniqueness and diversity but also has common values and principles that need to be followed and adhered to if we are to be effective and successful in fostering a sense of belonging.

The British values are: individual liberty, democracy, rule of law and mutual respect and tolerance of other faiths and beliefs. These values can be instilled into Early Years practice through the Early Years Foundation Stage curriculum and start with teaching children to take turns, negotiate, share, compromise and learn to resolve conflict in a responsible and fair way. This needs the whole community on board. It cannot be the sole responsibility of the practitioner and parents. It must involve the whole community and so the child needs to be visible to the meaningful neighbour, who also needs to follow the British values.

Finally, practitioners need to access honest facts as their values and opinions will influence children. As role models for the youngest generation, it is our duty and responsibility to have a positive impact on their development by creating an inclusive environment, building positive relationships and valuing uniqueness.

The best way to implement British values is by planning activities and routines that build the values in to daily practice. It also asks the practitioner to be a competent and true reflective practitioner by asking such questions as:

- Do I include all children and families in the setting?
- Do I celebrate difference?
- Do I access honest information and reflect on my own opinions and values, realising they may have an impact on my practice?
- Do I provide opportunities for children to have time to learn how to effectively work and play alongside each other, even in the smallest tasks and learn skills such as negotiating, compromising and resolving conflict from an early age so that they can grow to become responsible and caring citizens of the future?
- Do I ensure that children in my care are kept safe and am I aware of the safeguarding issues that can have a tremendous negative impact on children such as extremism that can lead to isolation and rejection?

The role of the practitioner is not easy. There are many challenges and issues facing Early Years settings. Children need strong attachments to form their own strong attachments. They have rights from birth and adults need to support their rights and recognise 'early childhood is a critical period for the realization of these rights' (UNICEF 2006: 1).

Practitioners need to foster a real and true sense of belonging for children in the Early Years if they are to be emotionally intelligent with a good self-esteem and care and regard for each other.

Bibliography

Allegretti, A (2015) Nine of the most surprising facts about immigration, *The Huffington Post.* Available from www.huffingtonpost.co.uk/2015/07/.../immigration-facts-surprising_n_7906122. html

An Everyday Story (n.d.) What is the Reggio Emilia approach? Available from http://www.anevery-daystory.com/beginners-guide-to-reggio-emilia/main-principles/

Black, J (2016) Celebrating British multiculturalism, lamenting England/Britain's past. *Nations and Nationalism* 22(4): 786–802. Available from www.researchgate.net/publication/299846384_Celebrating_British_multiculturalism_lamenting_EnglandBritain's_past

Bowcott, O and Adams, R (2016) Human rights group condemns Prevent anti-radicalisation strategy. *The Guardian*, 13th July 2016. Available from https://www.theguardian.com/politics/2016/jul/13/human-rights-group-condemns-prevent-anti-radicalisation-strategy

Bowlby, J (1969) *Attachment and loss.* New York: Basic Books.

Brodie, K (2014) *Sustained shared thinking in the Early Years linking theory to practice.* London: Routledge.

Bronfenbrenner, U (1979) *The ecology of human development: experiments by nature and design.* Harvard: Harvard University Press.

The Children Act (2004) Available from www.legislation.gov.uk/ukpga/2004/31/contents

The Children Society (2016) *Good childhood report.* Available from http://www.childrenssociety.org.uk/what-we-do/research/the-good-childhood-report

Crain, WC (1985) *Theories of development.* Prentice-Hall.

Department for Education for Children, Families and Schools (DfE) (2007) *Primary national strategy: supporting children learning English as an additional language Guidance for practitioners in the Early Years Foundation Stage.* Nottingham DCSF publications. Available from http://www.standards.dcsf.gov.uk/

Department for Education (DfE) (2011) *EAL pupils in schools: The latest statistics about EAL learners in our schools.* Available from https://www.naldic.org.uk/research-and-information/eal-statistics/eal-pupils/

Department for Education (DfE) (2014a) *Promoting fundamental British values as part of SMSC in schools Departmental advice for maintained schools.* London: TSO.

Department for Education (DfE) (2014b) *Statutory framework for the Early Years Foundation Stage.* Available from www.foundationyears.org.uk/eyfs-statutory-framework/

Department for Education (DfE) (2015a) *Keeping children safe in education: statutory guidance for schools and colleges.* London: TSO.

Department for Education (DfE) (2015b) *The prevent duty departmental advice for schools and childcare providers*. London: TSO.

Department for Education (DfE) (2016) *Keeping Children Safe in Education*. Available from https://www.gov.uk/government/uploads/system/uploads/attachment_data/file/550511/Keeping_children_safe_in_education.pdf

Department for Education (DfE) (2017) *Statutory framework for the Early Years Foundation Stage*. Available from http://www.foundationyears.org.uk/files/2017/03/EYFS_STATUTORY_FRAMEWORK_2017.pdf

Dowling, M (2013) *Young children's thinking*. London: Sage.

Dustmann, C and Frattini, T (2013) The fiscal effects of immigration to the UK. *The Economic Journal*, DOI: 10.1111/ecoj.12181. Available from www.cream-migration.org/publ_uploads/CDP_22_13.pdf.

Education and Inspections Act 2006, Chapter 40. London: TSO. Available from www.legisaltion.gov.uk/ukpga/2006/40/contents

Every Generation (n.d.) William Cuffay. Available from www.100greatblackbritons.com/bios/william_cuffay.html

Fox, T (2016) Four-year-old who mispronounced 'cucumber' as 'cooker bomb' faced terror warnings. *The Independent*, 12 March 2016. Available from http://www.independent.co.uk/news/uk/home-news/four-year-old-raises-concerns-of-radicalisation-after-pronouncing-cucumber-as-cooker-bomb-a6927341.html

Freire, P (1998) *Pedagogy of freedom: ethics, democracy, and civic courage*. Maryland: Rowman & Littlefield Publishers.

Freire, P (2005) *Pedagogy of the oppressed*. London: Penguin.

Goddard, C (2016) All about British values. *Nursery World*, 8–21 February: 25–28.

Goleman, D (1998) *Working with emotional intelligence*. New York: Bantam Dell.

Goleman, D (2006) *Social intelligence the new science of human relationships*. London: Random House.

Goorwich, S (2015) Old people's homes: everything that is right in the world. Available from http://metro.co.uk/2015/06/23/this-nursery-in-an-old-peoples-home-is-everything-thats-right-with-the-world-5261086/

Government Equalities Office and Equality and Human Rights Commission (2013, updated 2015) Information and guidance on the Equality Act 2010, including age discrimination and public sector Equality Duty. Available from https://www.gov.uk/guidance/equality-act-2010-guidance

Gregory, P (2015) *Doreen Lawrence*. Available from http://www.blackpresence.co.uk/?s=doreen+lawrence

The Guardian (2016) The propaganda of British values is a distortion of history. Available from https://www.theguardian.com/commentisfree/video/2016/oct/05/akala-the-propaganda-of-british-values-is-a-distortion-of-history-video

HM Government (2011) Prevent strategy. London: TSO.

HM Government (2012) *Channel: vulnerability assessment framework*. London: TSO.

HM Government (2015a) *Revised Prevent duty guidance for England and Wales*. London: TSO.

HM Government (2015b) *What to do if you're worried a child is being abused: advice for practitioners*. London: TSO.

HM Government (2015c) *Information Sharing: Advice for professionals providing safeguarding services to children, young people, parents and carers*. London: TSO.

HM Government (2015d) Counter Terrorism and Security Act 2015, Chapter 6. London: TSO. Available from: www.legislation.gov.uk/ukpga/2015/6

HM Government (2015e) *Working Together to Safeguard Children*. Available from https://www.gov.uk/government/uploads/system/uploads/attachment_data/file/592101/Working_Together_to_Safeguard_Children_20170213.pdf

Jones, O (2016) It's a cruel deceit to blame all our problems on immigration. *The Guardian*. Available from www.theguardian.com/commentisfree/2016/jun/09/cruel-deceit-problems-immigration-brexiters-truth

Laming, Lord (2003) The Victoria Climbié inquiry: report of an inquiry by Lord Laming. Available from http://victoria-climbie-inquiry.org.uk/

Lindon, J (2005) *Understanding child development: linking theory and practice*. London: Hodder Arnold Publication.

Lindon, J (2012) *Reflective practice and Early Years professionalism: linking theory and practice*. London: Hodder Education.

London Safeguarding Children Board (2016) See http://www.londonscb.gov.uk/

Merton Safeguarding Children's Board (n.d.) *Preventing radicalisation and extremism*. Available from: http://www.merton.gov.uk/mscb_prevent_guidance_final.pdf

Ministry of Education (2016) *Te Whāriki: He whāriki mātauranga mō ngā mokopuna o Aotearoa, Early childhood curriculum*. New Zealand Government. Available from https://education.govt.nz/assets/Documents/Early-Childhood/te-whariki.pdf

Morton, K (2014) *Children centre staff trained to spot signs of FGM*. Available from: www.nurseryworld.co.uk/nursery-world/news/1147497/children-centre-staff-trained-spot-signs-fgm

Moyles, J (2007) *Early Years foundations meeting the challenge*. Berkshire, England: Open University Press.

NatCen (2014) *British Social Attitudes report 33*. Available from http://www.bsa.natcen.ac.uk/latest-report/british-social-attitudes-33/introduction.aspx

NALDIC (National Association for Language Development In the Curriculum) (2012) See www.naldic.org.uk

Northern Ireland Assembly (2008) Implementation of the UNCRC by the UK: NGO alternative report. Available from http://archive.niassembly.gov.uk/io/research/2008/8508.pdf

NSPCC (2014a) *People whose first language is not English: learning from case reviews. Summary of risk factors and learning for improved practice around people whose first language is not English*. Available from www.nspcc.org.uk/preventing-abuse/child-protection-system/case-reviews/learning/first-language-not-english/

NSPCC (2014b) *Culture and faith: learning from case reviews*. Available from www.nspcc.org.uk/preventing-abuse/child-protection-system/case-reviews/learning/culture-faith/

The Nutbrown Review (2012) *Foundations for quality: the independent review of early education and childcare qualifications*. Available from www.gov.uk/government/uploads/system/uploads/attachment_data/file/175463/Nutbrown-Review.pdf

O'Caroll, L (2016) Ringleader of Rotherham child sexual abuse gang jailed for 35 years. *The Guardian*, 26 February 2016. Available from www.theguardian.com/uk-news/2016/feb/26/three-brothers-jailed-over-rotherham-child-sexual-abuse

Office for National Statistics (2011) *2011 Census*. Available from https://www.ons.gov.uk/census/2011census

Ofsted (2003) *Provision and support for Traveller pupils HMI 455*. Available from www.ofsted.gov.uk

Ofsted (2015a) *The common inspection framework: education, skills and early years*. London: TSO.

Ofsted (2015b) *Inspecting safeguarding in the Early Years, education, skills settings*. London: TSO.

Ofsted (2015c) *The Early Years inspection handbook*. London: TSO.

Oldham, J (2014) Trojan Horse: Park View School headteacher suspended. Available from www.birminghammail.co.uk/news/midlands-news/trojan-horse-park-view-headteacher-7510122

Osler, A and Starkey, H (2005) *Changing citizenship: democracy and inclusion in education.* Maidenhead: Open University Press.

Paley, VG (2008) *Vivian Gussin Paley at 92Y Wonderplay Conference 2008.* Available from www.youtube.com/watch?v=wWxYRkmHNXM

Park, E and King, K (2003) *Eric Digest cultural diversity and language socialisation in the early years.* Available at http://wwww.cal.org/resources/digest_pdfs/0313park.pdf

Piaget, J (1965) *Moral judgement on the child.* New York: Free Press.

Pfaff, W (2005) A monster of our own making. *The Observer*, August 2005.

Prevent duty guidance (2015) See www.safeguardinginschools.co.uk/wp-content/uploads/2015/04/PREVENT-Duty-Guidance-2015-03-09.pdf

Professional Association for Childcare and Early Years (PACEY) (2015) *Common inspection framework, British values and you.* Kent: PACEY.

Pugh, G and Duffy, B (2014) *Contemporary issues in the Early Years*, 6th edition. London: Sage.

Robson, J (2015) Fundamental British values in the early years – a dilemma for the sector. Available from http://www.consider-ed.org.uk/fundamental-british-values-in-the-early-years-a-dilemma-for-the-sector/

Rogers, CR (1959) 'A theory of therapy, personality, and interpersonal relationships, as developed in the client-centered framework' in S. Koch (Ed), *Psychology: A Study of a Science: Vol. 3* (pp. 184–256). New York, NY: McGraw-Hill.

Rosen, M (2014) Dear Mr Gove: what's so British about your British values? *The Guardian.* Available from: www.theguardian.com/education/2014/jul01/gove-what-is-so-british-your-british-values.

Rushworth, C (2010) *Vanessa George case review – Lessons to be learned.* Available from www.nurseryworld.co.uk/nursery-world/news/1095440/vanessa-george-review-lessons-learned

Sancisi, L and Edgington, M (2015) *Developing high quality observations, assessments and planning in the early years made to measure.* London and New York: Routledge.

Sargent, M (2016) *Promoting fundamental British values in the Early Years: a guide to the prevent duty and meeting the expectations of the new Common inspection framework practical pre-school books.* London: MA Education Ltd.

ScienceDaily (2014) Fear of terrorism increases resting heart rate, risk of death. Available from https://www.sciencedaily.com/releases/2014/12/141222165443.htm.

Sherwood, H (2016) People of no religion outnumber Christians in England and Wales – study. *The Guardian.* Available from www.theguardian.com/world/2016/may/23/no-religionoutnumber-christians-england-wales-study

Smith, A (1993) *A national identity*, new edition. Aylesbury: FORTIUS Ltd.

Smith, MK (2016) 'What is teaching?' in *The Encyclopaedia of Informal Education.* Available from http://infed.org/mobi/what-is-teaching/

Sylvw, K, Melhuish, E, Sammons, P, Siraj-Blatchford, I, and Taggart, B (2004) The Effective Provision of Preschool Education (EPPE) project. Findings from pre-school to end of Key Stage 1. Available from http://eppe.ioe.ac.uk/eppe/eppepdfs/RBTec1223sept0412.pdf

Tassoni, P (2014) *Early Years educator for the work based learner.* London: Hodder.

Travellers Times (n.d.) Events. Available from http://travellerstimes.org.uk/Events.aspx

UNCRC (2015) United Nations Convention on the Rights of the Child. See https://www.lgbtyouth.org.uk/m/news/uncrc-report-2015

UNICEF (2006) *The Convention on the Rights of the Child, September 2005*. Available from https://www.unicef-irc.org/portfolios/general_comments/GC7.Rev.1_en.doc.html

UNICEF (2016) *United Nations on the rights of the child: children's rights and responsibilities*. New York: UNICEF Publications. Available from www.unicef.org/rightsite/files/rights_leaflet.pdf

United Nations Human Rights Officer of the Rights Commission (2016) Statement by the United Nations Special Rapporteur on the rights to freedom of peaceful assembly and of association at the conclusion of his visit to the United Kingdom. Available from www.ohchr.org/EN/News Events/Pages/DisplayNews.aspx?NewsID=19854&LangID=E#sthash.9dqLAK5F.dpuf

University of Leicestershire (2006) Gang Culture. Available from www.le.ac.uk/ebulletin-archive/ebulletin/features/2000-2009/2006/08/nparticle.2006-08-03.html

Wiltshire, R and Burn, D (2009) *Growing in the community,* second edition. Available from www.local.gov.uk/c/document_library/get_file?uuid=28d8ca84–9f61-4550-9c84-6e9d04b-da872&groupId=10180)

Index

Page numbers in bold denote tables. Page numbers in italics denote figures.